CALIFORNIA
Ghost notes

Haunted Happenings
Throughout
the Golden State

As recorded by
Randall A. Reinstedt

Ghost Town Publications
Carmel, California

If bookstores in your area do not carry *California Ghost Notes*, copies may be obtained by writing to . . .

Ghost Town Publications
P.O. Drawer 5998
Carmel, CA 93921

www.ghosttownpub.com

For other books by Randall A. Reinstedt see page 248.

Photos on pages 109–130 are the property of their respective owners (see Photo Credits section, page 242).

10 9 8 7 6 5

Manufactured in the United States of America

ISBN 978-0-933818-10-1
Library of Congress Control Number: 00-134941

Edited by John Bergez
Cover and map by Ed Greco
Typesetting by Erick and Mary Ann Reinstedt

CALIFORNIA

Ghost
notes

*This book is dedicated to those
who have gone before*

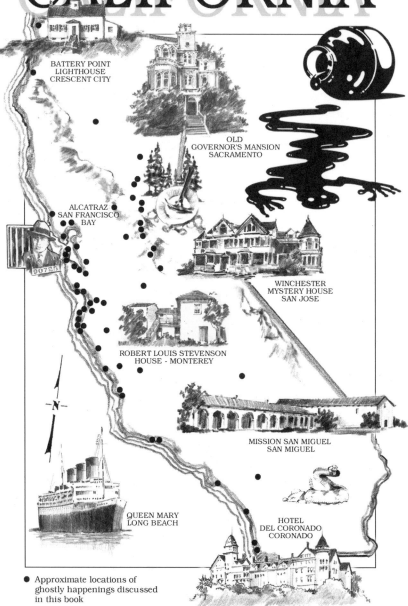

CALIFORNIA

BATTERY POINT
LIGHTHOUSE
CRESCENT CITY

OLD
GOVERNOR'S MANSION
SACRAMENTO

ALCATRAZ
SAN FRANCISCO
BAY

WINCHESTER
MYSTERY HOUSE
SAN JOSE

ROBERT LOUIS STEVENSON
HOUSE - MONTEREY

-N-

MISSION SAN MIGUEL
SAN MIGUEL

QUEEN MARY
LONG BEACH

HOTEL
DEL CORONADO
CORONADO

● Approximate locations of
ghostly happenings discussed
in this book

Contents

CALIFORNIA

Ghost

notes

Introduction

If you are familiar with any of my other ghost books, you know that I'm not a ghost hunter. I'm not obsessed with the supernatural, and I don't claim any special expertise about things that go bump in the night. Perhaps most important of all, I have never seen a ghost! Yet ghost stories have a way of finding me, as they do anyone who probes into the vast store of California lore. Along with countless other accounts of the strange and unexplained, ghostly tales are an important part of the history and culture of the Golden State. In the eighty-plus sections of this book, you'll discover accounts of more than one hundred separate incidents, many of them published here for the first time. Along the way, you'll also find quite a bit of information about a number of California's historic places and colorful characters.

It's really the connection with history that explains how I began collecting and recording ghost stories. I'm a former teacher and lifelong history buff who believes that the best way to make history come alive is through stories. Over a period of more than thirty years, I've assembled a wealth of tales and odd bits of information on a variety of fascinating subjects, including buried treasures, dramatic shipwrecks, mysterious sea monsters, plundering pirates, brazen bandits, and lost gold mines. Along the way, I became a kind of archivist of anecdotes and little-known incidents, many of them related to me by the people who experienced them. To me, all these stories are

1

part of California's legends and lore, and all combine to make history exciting and fun to learn about.

Stories of ghosts and other peculiar happenings were stirred into the mix right from the beginning. It all began in 1970, when my home town of Monterey was celebrating its 200th birthday. I was asked to write an article about the aged adobes of California's first capital city and the part they had played in its history. After I agreed to the project, I thought, "These buildings have been written about so many times, how can I make my account different and interesting?" It was then that I got to thinking about growing up in Monterey and hearing all the exciting stories about the ghosts, bandits, and treasures that were connected with its old buildings. "That's it," I thought, "that's the answer: I'll tell some of these tales, and slip in a little about the history of these structures along the way."

The result was terrific! After adding to the accounts I already knew by interviewing as many old-timers and docents that I could, I ended up with enough information for a two-part magazine article. It was called "Ghosts of Old Monterey," and, for all intents and purposes, that was the beginning of my quest for ghost stories.

As it turned out, even in the expanded two-part article, I wasn't able to include all of the accounts that I had collected. It was because of this, along with the interest the article had generated, that I decided to add a few more tales and bring out a small book for those who were curious about Monterey's ghosts. Also called *Ghosts of Old Monterey,* the book was quite a success. Not only did it sell out, but I started getting phone calls from people who wanted to share their experiences about ghosts as well as other local happenings. It wasn't long before I revised and updated the original book and came out with an expanded version called *Ghosts, Bandits and Legends of Old Monterey.* Thirty years later, after numerous printings and a major revision in 1995, the book is still going strong.

The success of *Ghosts, Bandits and Legends* led not only to several other books (see page 248 for a partial list), but also to many more tales about the strange and unexplained. Even with five ghost books behind me, by the 1990s I still had enough material in my files to publish my largest ghost book yet. It was called *Ghost Notes: Haunted Happenings on California's Historic Monterey Peninsula*. As the title implies, the book was a gathering of tales in the form of relatively brief notes, presented in the order in which I learned about them. Most of the accounts had never been published before, and, as the subtitle indicates, most of the incidents took place on or near the Monterey Peninsula.

The success of *Ghost Notes* was truly gratifying. And, as you have probably guessed, it was the writing of this publication that eventually led to *California Ghost Notes*. It so happened that about the time I started putting *Ghost Notes* together, I was also involved in writing a series of books for children about California history. The books are used primarily in schools around the state at the fourth grade level. In this capacity I often traveled to different parts of California, giving talks, doing research, and attending conferences. With the success of *Ghost Notes* very much on my mind, and my interest in ghosts revived, I often asked about ghosts in the various places I visited. Many of the accounts in this book are the result of those casual questions. Numerous other tales come from customers at conferences who visited our Ghost Town Publications booth. Many others, of course, come from a variety of printed sources as well as personal interviews. As I indicated at the start of this introduction, you don't have to be a ghost hunter to accumulate an amazing variety of "supernatural" tales. Once people know that you're sincerely interested in their tales and experiences, it seems that ghosts start hunting *you!*

I am proud to say that in most cases—regardless of how I obtained the stories—I have visited the buildings or sites that are discussed in this book. Not only that, but more often than not the accounts presented here have been shared with me by the very people who experienced them. In this connection, I want to make it clear that I have *purposely* chosen to omit the names of my sources so that I won't be responsible for their being hounded by the curious (or by those who want to sensationalize their stories). For similar reasons I don't pinpoint private residences or business establishments whose owners don't want the structures to be known as haunted. Of course, I do identify public buildings and those of a historic nature.

As you make your way through this volume, particularly in the earlier sections, you will see that the Monterey Peninsula is well represented, as it is in my other ghost books. That's partly because the stories are presented in chronological order, and my search for ghost stories expanded across the state as this project developed. Another reason is that it seems like almost everywhere I go in this beautiful place, people seek me out and want to share incidents that they have experienced or that they have heard about from their family and friends. I think you'll agree that a good story is worth reading (and retelling) no matter where it happened to take place. You'll also find, though, that this book covers many regions of California, including both well-known sites like Alcatraz and the *Queen Mary* as well as a number of locations that are off the beaten path. If you're so inclined, you can use this book as a kind of field guide for a ghostly tour of the Golden State—whether in person, or in the comfort of your armchair (and your imagination). Most of all, I hope you'll enjoy following my own journey of discovery by reading the accounts I have compiled over the last decade in the order in which I recorded them.

Now, almost ten years after I put the finishing touches on the original *Ghost Notes*, it seems clear that ghosts are—if you'll excuse the pun—alive and well. We may not know exactly what lies behind the strange and often eerie experiences that so many people have reported, but the incidents themselves show that there is definitely *something* going on out there!

In case you have any doubt about that, consider this. I have no reason to question the sincerity of the vast majority of the people who have shared their tales with me. But suppose that half or even three-quarters of the tales that I have recorded in this text are fictitious. In fact, suppose that 99 percent of the incidents I've described are merely people's imaginations gone astray. We would still be left with one percent, or, more simply put, at least one account that defies all doubt. Certainly, of the more than one hundred incidents I've described in this book, you can find one that works for you and that has the feel of authenticity to it. Now, even if only that single, unexplainable incident did, in fact, happen, I think you'd have to agree that something we can only describe as supernatural *is* taking place.

For myself, I can only say that the people who have shared their experiences with me over the last thirty-plus years—including, among others, doctors, lawyers, priests, police officers, and other responsible and respected citizens—can't *all* be liars, or hallucinating. And it's a fair bet that *whatever* is going on is continuing to happen even as I write these words. If there's anything I've learned over the years, it's that there is no way to write "the end" to the story of ghosts and mysterious happenings!

CALIFORNIA

Ghost

notes

California Ghost Notes

Ghosts hanging around . . .

July 29, 1990 While I was enjoying a Feast of the Lanterns gathering in Pacific Grove (a small community that neighbors Monterey), a delightful couple sought me out. They were familiar with my ghost books, and they had a couple of stories they wanted to share with me.

The lady was the first to speak. She told me about a frightening, humanlike figure that she saw "on several occasions" in her garage, hanging by the neck! The figure was dressed in a cloak or a type of hooded cape. It was visible only at certain times and, apparently, could only be seen by her.

In asking around, the lady learned that a man had hung himself in a garage a short distance away, though none of her neighbors knew of a similar incident having taken place at her address. When she told a trusted friend and co-worker about the sighting, the friend, who was of Hawaiian descent, taught her how to perform certain rituals used by Hawaiians to rid their houses of spirits. After several attempts in which she followed the elaborate rituals, the mysterious figure vanished . . . never to return.

A second account was told by the lady's gentleman friend. Like his companion, he was probably in his late thirties. It seems that when he was connected with the army, he was assigned to the Salinas Armory. (Salinas, which is a short distance inland from Monterey, is known as, among many other things, the home of writer John Steinbeck.) While he was at the armory, he heard a number of stories about the ghost of a soldier who had committed suicide by hanging himself behind the stage in the facility. Not long after the soldier's death, his ghostly presence began to be felt, along with a "cold spot" that appeared with it. (As you may know, cold spots are thought to be where a spirit enters or exits a building or room.) My informant described how he had experienced both these phenomena, as he had been roused from his sleeping bag by the presence and its associated cold spot.

Probably the best-known incident at the Salinas Armory took place when a group of Boy Scouts were using the facility. As the story goes, late one night, when most of the younger scouts were asleep, a group of the older boys—who had managed to smuggle in some booze—broke out the bottles and began to party. Their festivities came to a screeching halt, however, when the bottles were mysteriously knocked from their hands! If that wasn't enough to convince them that they were doing the wrong thing in the wrong place, the next happening certainly did the trick. Suddenly their cots began to collapse, as if an invisible something went from bed to bed, knocking the legs out from under them! At that point they could be sure that the ghost of the dead soldier was not happy with their shenanigans.

She "wasn't really there" . . .

October 29, 1990 After my "Halloween" talk to a group of prospective teachers, a young woman came up and asked if she could share some of her experiences with me. Pulling up a chair to the table where I had been autographing books, she sat down and proceeded to tell me about three incidents she had experienced. Of most interest to me was a happening that took place in a large, abandoned, Spanish-style structure in world-famous Pebble Beach.

The young lady explained that when she was a teenager, she and four of her friends (two girls and two boys) went to the house to see what they could see. At that time, the building was known among local teens as "the haunted house." It was foreboding in appearance and had been empty for many years. Being new to the area, the then-teenager was fascinated by the building and the stories that went with it. One of the tales told about a young boy who had suffocated in an upstairs bedroom.

In the dark of night, the teenagers explored the house by the light of the moon. As they ventured upstairs, one of the boys (who had been there before) acted as a guide. It was he who had told the others about the tragedy connected with the house, and it was he who now led his companions to the boy's bedroom.

While they were in the bedroom, the young woman told me, she was suddenly overcome by an "icy" feeling. At the same instant, she saw the vague outline of what appeared to be a towel or piece of white cloth hanging in the air, almost as if it were draped over something. When she reached out and touched the object, it vanished! At that instant, a peculiar—almost sickly—feeling came over her. An urgent urge to vomit drove her from the room, and it was all she could do to get out of the house before she became ill. After throwing up, she slipped into "a kind of trance," feeling as if she "wasn't really there."

Her friends were naturally very concerned about what was taking place, especially since they couldn't seem to bring her back to reality. Wisely, they took her home. By the time she reached her house, she was feeling a little better. Nevertheless, she went straight to bed.

After a restless night, and still feeling poorly the next morning, the frightened teenager went to see a doctor. A thorough check revealed nothing wrong . . . except that she had a very low temperature. This bothered the doctor, who suggested rest and observation for the next few days. It wasn't until about two weeks later that she began to feel like her old self.

Years later, the young lady is still perplexed by what overcame her as she reached out to touch the towel-like cloth. With wide eyes, she admits to wondering whether the presence that haunts the boy's room had somehow passed from the ghostly image to her when she touched the mysterious object.

A restless recluse . . .

October 30, 1990 Earlier this month, I got a call from a reporter inquiring about a house in Carmel that boasted several ghostly happenings. Being unfamiliar with the accounts, and unable to add to her collection of tales, I forgot about the call until I read today's paper. After learning more of the story, I thought it would be interesting to add to my *Ghost Notes* file.

According to the account, a young couple recently moved into a Carmel dwelling of 1920s vintage. (Carmel, officially known as Carmel-by-the-Sea, is the charming community nestled in the forest by Carmel Bay, just south of Monterey.) Unexplainable happenings—such as the couple's bed shaking in the middle of the night—began to occur almost immediately. Numerous other odd events soon followed. Among the incidents were windows and doors slamming shut by themselves, heavy footsteps heard when no one else was there, bathroom faucets turning on when the room was empty, paper items found scattered about a room, cold spots (or drafts) felt in various locations, scraping sounds heard in the living room, a mysterious shape appearing in front of the television, and the sighting of an old man's face in the bedroom.

Concerned and more than a little scared, the couple had the building blessed by a local priest. Next, they contacted a paranormal investigator from the San Francisco Bay Area. After checking into the history of the house, the investigator and his helpers learned that a reclusive gentleman who had lived there had recently died. Further checking revealed that the man's wife and son had also died while staying at the house.

Thinking that the troubled spirit of the man might continue to linger at the structure, the investigator returned to the house with a message for its former resident. He told the spirit that his son (who had been retarded) was happy. He also said that there was no need for the spirit to remain at the house and that he should go on to where he needed to be.

Since the investigator delivered these messages, the couple reported, the house has been relatively free of strange happenings. They plan to continue living in their now-peaceful Carmel hideaway.

While I am on the subject of Carmel hideaways, I'd like to touch on another structure in this charming bayside community. Situated on a side street on the south side of town, the building is well known to Carmelites. Made mostly of stone, it enjoys the distinctions of being one of the village's earliest inns and of having hosted an amazing number of important guests, especially from the field of literature. Local lore has it that the ghosts of several of these well-known writers (including Mary Austin, George Sterling, and Jack London) frequent the aged structure.

Author's Note: The newspaper article mentioned in this account is "A Halloween Ghost Story," by Carolyn Rice (*Monterey Peninsula Herald,* October 30, 1990). For a closer look at the delightful establishment mentioned at the end of this section, see "The feelings were strongest in George Sterling's room . . . ," page 97.

More restless spirits . . .

October 30, 1990 Interestingly, an article in a second Monterey Peninsula publication recently featured the same investigator mentioned in the last note. (Yes, it's almost Halloween, and time for strange tales.) This second article documented happenings at two additional structures on the Peninsula.

The first tale takes us back to Carmel, where a couple reported seeing several apparitions in their house. The first sightings were of a little boy running through the building. For a time the boy was seen on almost a daily basis; then the sightings stopped. They were followed, however, by mysterious knocks on the front door. When the door was opened, a middle-aged man was seen standing in the entryway . . . until he faded from sight. Finally the knockings ceased, but then the structure began to be frequented by an elderly man who had difficulty walking. He seemed to appear out of nowhere and proceeded to shuffle about the building.

As in the preceding Carmel account, the paranormal investigator learned that a former resident of the house had recently died. The investigator was able to track down a member of the deceased man's family in a neighboring community and bring this person to the house. After this visit, during which the family member encouraged the presence to "pass on," the Carmel couple experienced no further problems.

The second happening involves a couple who inherited a house in Monterey's Skyline Forest. Once again a previous occupant had recently died, a man who had taken pride in his garden. After moving into the house, the couple began finding garden tools scattered about. They also noticed dirt in the sink, as if someone had washed his hands there, and the movement of a variety of objects, including the deceased man's favorite chair. Unfortunately, these happenings are still occurring, as apparently the presence continues to putter about the place.

Author's Note: The article mentioned in this account is "Who You Gonna Call?" by Sharon Randall (*The Weekly Sun,* October 25, 1990).

Ghostly happenings at the Robert Louis Stevenson House . . .

May 25, 1991 As readers of some of my other books know, one of the Monterey buildings best known for ghostly happenings is the Robert Louis Stevenson House. The famed writer stayed in this structure for a short time in 1879, when it was known as the French Hotel. Today it is a part of the California state park system, and a favorite stop for visitors to old Monterey.

Today I met a lady who worked as a park attendant for the state's local parks and historic buildings in 1989. As we chatted about my ghost books, she told me about odd experiences she had had in certain state buildings, including the Soberanes Adobe (where objects would move mysteriously from place to place) and the Cooper Molera complex (where she experienced icy feelings and assorted cold spots, even on hot summer days). However, it was at the Stevenson House that most of the strange happenings took place.

As with the Soberanes Adobe, the most mystifying of these events was the frequent moving of objects in various rooms. The lady's duties at the Stevenson House included dusting and vacuuming. In this capacity she had access to the otherwise locked rooms. (At the time the house had cell-like doors or gates at the entrances to several of its rooms to keep guests from taking, or breaking, the many valuable items on display.) Being familiar with the stories of the ghostly Lady in Black and other tales associated with the building, she decided to make chalk marks showing the positions of objects in several rooms as she finished cleaning. Sure enough, the next day she would find that several of the objects had moved during the night—even though the building was locked and all the alarms were set.

Since my informant states that she was the last person to leave in the evening and the first to arrive the next day, I am at a loss to check out her story and can only add her experiences to the ever-growing list of Stevenson House tales. Certainly she is neither the first nor the last to report such things as furniture and other objects being moved about in unexplained ways.

I was also interested in a second account that this former park attendant shared with me. It seems that she learned of several odd occurrences that had taken place in the beautiful back gardens of the Stevenson House while she was working with the gardener there. One such happening that caused considerable frustration for the gardener was his inability to make certain plants grow despite his best efforts to follow the master plan for the garden. Try as he might, no amount of care, coaxing, or special fertilizers would make the plants grow, even though they were well-suited to the location and should have flourished. However, when he planted the kinds of plants that had been there before—and that had been placed there by a former gardener, a greatly respected man who had a genuine love for the house and its grounds—the plants grew in profusion and were admired by all who saw them.

Author's Note: An interesting postscript to this note on the Robert Louis Stevenson House concerns an encounter I had a couple of months later in a shop on Monterey's

---

Cannery Row, where a stack of my children's book *The Strange Case of the Ghosts of the Robert Louis Stevenson House* was on display. Suddenly a middle-aged gentleman picked up one of the books and remarked, "There really *are* ghosts at the Stevenson House."

Without disclosing that I was the book's author, I asked how he knew that there were ghosts there. He told me that he had heard a number of stories from one of the state park attendants who worked at the house. These accounts included such things as tales of objects "floating about" and stories of pillows and toys (mainly dolls) that mysteriously changed locations.

Haunted hotels . . .

October 14, 1991 With Halloween approaching, and news of the publication of *Ghost Notes* spreading about the Monterey Peninsula, I received a telephone call today that led to several tales. The caller was a young woman—I'd guess she was in her twenties—who represented a local radio station. It seems that some people at the station thought it would be fun to broadcast a Halloween show from a haunted house, and she was calling to locate such a house. She seemed to be quite knowledgeable about several strange happenings in the Monterey area, and we made plans to meet for coffee. As it turned out, she brought her roommate along, and the three of us had a delightful visit.

Among the stories she related were a number that concerned Monterey's old Hotel Del Monte, now the United States Naval Postgraduate School. Before recounting these tales, let me say a word about this historic establishment. The majestic Del Monte opened its doors in 1880, and in its heyday it was a magnet for the elite of the world, including (in its later years) a number of Hollywood stars. Some of its wealthy guests even arrived in their own railroad cars, while others rode in the public trains from San Francisco to this elegant seaside retreat. Over the years, the site has evidently become a magnet for ghosts, too, as any number of ghostly stories are told about it. (For a collection of such accounts, see my book *Incredible Ghosts of Old Monterey's Hotel Del Monte.*)

In addition to the main building, the Del Monte featured a number of cottages scattered about the grounds. Actually, the word "cottages" is somewhat misleading, as these structures are substantially larger than most people's image of a cottage. They were built after a 1924 fire destroyed much of the hotel. After the Del Monte was rebuilt, the cottages were used by guests who desired extra space and privacy. Today, many of the cottages house naval officers and their families.

Over the years, several interesting stories have been told about these buildings. One that I recounted in *Ghost Notes* tells about the sighting of Charlie Chaplin's ghost. The apparition was reported by two people, at different times, with neither knowing about the other sighting.

The young lady from the radio station had several incidents to add to the store of reported happenings at the old Del Monte. She told of a guard dog being picked up by some unseen thing, a ghostly presence that occasionally appears in an aged downstairs bank vault, and the apparition of a woman dancing in the ballroom. One amusing story concerned two Naval School employees who were on duty in the downstairs kitchen when the dumbwaiters started going up and down by themselves. Not waiting around for an explanation, the two workers immediately exited the area. Later, when they filled out forms to explain their absence, they both wrote the word "Ghosts!"

Another hotel-related story concerned a second establishment, the Hotel San Carlos, which was a Monterey landmark for more than half a century. (It was demolished in 1983 to make room for the Monterey Sheraton, now the Monterey Regency.) The old San Carlos featured an ornate fountain and a large fishpond near its entrance. It was here that the ghost of a little girl who resided at the hotel was often seen trying to catch the goldfish that lived in the pond.

Author's Note: Inasmuch as I mentioned famous Hollywood stars who once stayed and played at the grand old Hotel Del Monte, you might be curious to know who some of them were. Besides Charlie Chaplin, the celebrities who added to the Del Monte's glamour included such notables as Mary Pickford, Jackie Coogan, Greta Garbo, Will Rogers, Jean Harlow, Oliver Hardy, Darryl Zanuck, W. C. Fields, Mary Astor, Joe E. Brown, Ann Harding, Edward G. Robinson, Errol Flynn, Greer Garson, Clark Gable, Bing Crosby, Ava Gardner, Johnny Weismuller, Ginger Rogers, William Powell, Olivia De Haviland, Mickey Rooney, and Joan Fontaine.

A local psychic worked his magic . . .

October 27, 1991 As I mention in the Introduction to my book *Ghost Notes,* one never knows when one will learn of a ghostly happening. So perhaps it was appropriate that I heard this story following an autograph party for *Ghost Notes* at a local bookstore.

The tale comes from a middle-aged woman who had brought with her an envelope containing three pages of notes about strange happenings in her Carmel home. As we talked, she elaborated on some of the items she had jotted down.

The lady described a feeling of presence—"a sort of heaviness"—that permeated the home, and that she blamed for many of the things that took place there. These events included the somewhat typical "haunting" incidents of locked doors suddenly opening, water faucets being turned on, objects disappearing and reappearing just as mysteriously, and knocking sounds heard within the walls, usually at night near the woman's bed. But there were less common manifestations as well, such as terrible odors drifting about the house, doors locking by themselves (sometimes even trapping people in rooms), columns of smoke and "nebulous forms" appearing and disappearing, and a "rustling" of towels in the bathroom when all doors, windows, and vents were shut. My informant also reported finding assorted "gifts" (including money and small figurines) about the house, discovering long-lost objects between stacks of clothing that had been laid out only the day before, and engaging in a "tug of war" with a downstairs door.

The "grand finale" (as the lady called it) began when she was awakened from a dream by sounds that at first seemed to be part of the dream. As she lay in bed, fully awake, she realized that the sounds were very real, and that they were coming from her own bedroom. They included what she described as buzzing, crackling, and "electric" types of noises. She then saw a beautiful round form, measuring between three and four feet across, by the door of her bathroom. The form was a gorgeous, "sort of variegated" rose color. It didn't appear to be solid, and inside it were what seemed to be white and gold electric currents. The sounds appeared to be coming from this brilliant center section of the "form."

Eventually these events, and the continued feeling of heaviness in the house, prompted the woman to call for help. Happily for her, after a local psychic visited the dwelling and worked his magic, things began to settle down. Soon a light and airy ambiance settled about the house.

Incidentally, this house was built in 1931 and is a short three-block walk from downtown Carmel.

A phantom white mare . . .

November 13, 1991 Not all ghostly apparitions involve the spirits of human beings. I was reminded of this today when I stopped by an elderly friend's house in Pacific Grove for a chat and was rewarded with some delightful tales about her childhood. Having been born nearly ninety years ago on a ranch near the Monterey County community of Gonzales, she had a number of enjoyable stories to share that touched on the history of the Salinas Valley.

One "ghostly" anecdote concerned her first horse, a large white mare that she delighted in riding and caring for. The horse died when she was a young teenager, and its death brought her considerable sadness. However, these feelings did not last for long, for about two weeks after the animal's death, she saw it again! She was doing chores around the ranch house when she looked up and saw her mare trot out of a nearby canyon and make its way to a watering trough. Looking fit, the mare proceeded to drink its fill . . . and then vanish before her eyes!

That was the last my friend ever saw of her beloved horse. But whenever she thought of it again, it was no longer with sadness, because she knew that her mare was happy in its next life.

A ghost straight out of Steinbeck . . .

March 25, 1992 As I was leaving a coffeehouse in Pacific Grove, I was hailed by one of the customers, a young man I had chatted with before. He was quite anxious to tell me about a sighting that he and a lady friend had made near Monterey's famed Cannery Row.

As you may know, the Row is perhaps best known because of John Steinbeck's novel, *Cannery Row,* which was published in 1945. The "cannery" part of the name

19

dates back to the years when Monterey was known as the Sardine Capital of the World. In the era of the 1930s, thousands of people were employed in the local sardine fishing industry. Many of them labored in the fish canneries that lined the waterfront on a street known as Ocean View Avenue. Because of the popularity of Steinbeck's novel, in 1958 the City of Monterey officially changed the name of the street to Cannery Row.

There are echoes of this history in the tale the young man had to tell me. It seems that about a month ago, he and his companion were driving down David Avenue in the area locals refer to as New Monterey. As they neared Cannery Row, they spotted the ghostly figure of an old man staggering up the avenue, looking as if he had had too much to drink. Wearing high boots (probably rubber), jeans, and a leather jacket, the figure looked like the cannery workers they had seen depicted in old photographs. As the couple slowed down to take a closer look, they noticed that the aged fellow was unshaven and that his eyes appeared bleary. Abruptly the ghostly figure vanished from sight.

In reflecting on this incident, my informant offered the thought that perhaps the worker was "a character out of Steinbeck's *Cannery Row*." Referring to Steinbeck's friend and drinking mate, Ed "Doc" Ricketts, he added with a laugh, "Maybe the ghost had just left Doc's, and had been drinking with 'old John' himself."

Hattie lives . . .

March 26, 1992 As the saying goes, when it rains, it pours. Today brought a couple of unexpected conversations about ghostly happenings, oddly enough involving the same location.

As I was sipping a cup of coffee at one my favorite Pacific Grove spots, jotting down my recollections about the Cannery Row ghost I heard about yesterday, a friend stopped by my table. Out of the blue, he announced that Hattie Gragg was still "doing her thing" at the Stokes Adobe.

As readers of some of my previous ghost books know, the Stokes Adobe was built in the 1830s and today is a popular Monterey restaurant. Hattie Gragg lived in the building from the 1890s to the 1940s, and it is her ghost that is usually blamed for the many odd occurrences that are reported to take place there. Over the years Hattie has been accused of such things as playing the piano, tinkling the chandeliers, moving a variety of objects (including a large candelabra in the bar), and turning lights and music systems on and off.

My friend's information did not include anything that I hadn't already written about, but later in the day a second acquaintance stopped me as I was picking up my mail in Carmel. He asked whether my latest book (*Ghost Notes*) had any Stokes Adobe happenings in it. Assuring him that it did, I asked why he had a sudden interest in the building. In reply, he told me about a conversation with a waiter that he had there a couple of nights ago. The waiter told him about an odd experience involving the place settings at the tables in his station. After patiently setting up the tables, the waiter had left the room for a brief time. Upon his return, all of the table settings had been changed! The station in question was his to set up, and he was sure that no one had been near it when the changes took place. Interestingly, at the time this incident took place, the waiter was new to the area and unfamiliar with any ghost stories connected with the building.

They were greeted by a human skeleton . . .

May 20, 1992 I heard a new story this evening about a building I've written briefly about before, the "Captain's

House." This structure is an aged Victorian located in Pacific Grove. The story comes from a gentleman (perhaps in his sixties) whom I met while signing books in the San Joaquin Valley town of Ceres, near the city of Modesto. As we were chatting about the man's fond memories of the Monterey Peninsula, he told me about visiting the Captain's House many years before, long before I had ever been there. I asked about his experiences there, and he proceeded to tell me one of the most interesting and unnerving tales I have heard about the house.

It seems that this gentleman became friends with an older lady who lived in the dwelling, and she shared several stories with him. One of them concerned an incident that had happened some years before, when she decided to change the wallpaper in the kitchen. Along with some helpers, she began stripping the old paper off the wall. This task turned out to be more of a job than she had anticipated because there were several layers of paper to remove.

When she and her helpers finally reached the original surface, they noticed the outline of an opening that had been cut into the wall. The opening appeared to be a door, but there were no signs of hinges or a doorknob. Curious about why the opening had been put there, they checked the back side of the wall and found a closet that apparently had a false rear wall blocking the space where the opening should have led. Now there was no holding them back, and they began the task of removing the door from the kitchen wall.

It was then that they got the shock of their lives. When they removed the secret door, they were greeted by a human skeleton!

Whose skeleton it was, and why it was concealed in the wall, the woman never learned. But this episode certainly gives new meaning to the many stories that have been told about the house, such as the sightings, many years ago, of the ghostly figure of an aged ship captain pacing to and fro on the building's balcony.

The poor fellow met an untimely end . . .

May 22, 1992 As I was chatting with a mechanic friend of mine—he is nearly seventy and has been working on my cars since the 1950s—we got to talking about his boyhood days on Cannery Row. Having been part of the scene when the sardine was king, and John Steinbeck and Ed "Doc" Ricketts were holding forth, he has some fond memories of the Row and of the characters who frequented the area.

One such person was a Chinese gentleman who lived in a building one block above the cannery-lined street. Unfortunately, my mechanic friend related, the poor fellow met an untimely end, as somebody entered the building and killed him by striking him about the head.

What aroused my interest about this incident was that I had written about this very structure in my *Ghost Notes* book. The tale I recounted there concerned a local gentleman who operates a restaurant in the building. When the establishment first opened, this man was troubled by a distinct and disturbing feeling of presence. The "presence" was felt only at certain times, and then only by certain people. Not knowing what to make of these feelings, the owner had the building checked out by two psychics. Interestingly, this duo reported picking up "strong vibes" in the building and indicated that not one, but two people had died there. One, they said, died "an alcoholic's death," while the other—they thought—had been murdered in the structure.

It is this second death that comes to mind now as I think of my mechanic's tale. Could the psychics have been picking up on the murder of the Chinese gentleman? If so,

I can only tip my cap to two people with an uncanny ability to look into the past.

The money had vanished . . .

June 5, 1992 As I was browsing through a local bookstore yesterday, the manager waved a copy of *Ghost Notes* at me and said I should talk to one of his workers, who had recently experienced a ghostly happening at one of Pacific Grove's bed and breakfast inns. Later I was introduced to the young lady, whom I will call Lucy. It turned out that she did indeed have an interesting tale to tell.

Lucy explained that she worked as a night clerk and hostess at the inn, which boasts a colorful past and is one of Pacific Grove's most historic structures. Even though she had only worked there a short time and felt "uncomfortable" in certain parts of the place, it was obvious that she was excited about the job and generally enjoyed her work.

The uncomfortable feelings that Lucy experienced stemmed from the main entryway and the side bedroom that was originally connected to it. When the building was converted into an inn, the door connecting the entryway and bedroom was sealed, and an outside entrance to the bedroom was built. Except for the "strong feelings of presence" in these two areas, the rest of the house was warm and inviting. Lucy worked as quickly as possible in the rooms where she felt uneasy and kept her feelings to herself until something happened that caused her to seek out the inn's manager.

The incident occurred when she was turning down the beds in the bedroom that had originally been connected to the entryway. Upon entering the room, Lucy noticed a crumpled dollar bill on the hardwood floor near the bed. Having been instructed never to touch guests' belongings—especially their money—she made a point of staying

24

clear of the bill as she hurriedly began her task of turning down the bed. Before walking around the bed to turn down the other side, she glanced at the bill, which was still on the floor. However, when she came back to that side of the bed, the money had vanished! Not wanting to be blamed for having taken it, Lucy got down on her hands and knees and searched for the missing bill. With the money nowhere in sight and the feeling of presence getting stronger and stronger, she exited the room and sought out the manager.

After hearing Lucy's tale, the manager told her not to worry and assured her that the money would be there when she returned to the room. He then described other strange happenings connected with the bedroom and the entryway, adding that he would appreciate it if Lucy kept these incidents to herself so as not to "spook" the cleaning ladies.

Later Lucy went back to the bedroom, and sure enough, there was the dollar bill on the floor, exactly where she had last seen it! I asked about drafts that could have caused the bill to move, but she assured me that she had checked for open doors and windows at the time and that there were no drafts in the room.

Upon further checking, Lucy learned that one of the inn's owners (a woman who had lived in the building for more than fifteen years) had also felt the "presence." Not only that, but she had reported seeing the ghostly figure of what she thought was the original owner in the main entryway.

One reason I find this story interesting is that I had previously written about this structure in my book *Ghostly Tales and Mysterious Happenings of Old Monterey*. Among the items I recorded there was one involving a man who had supposedly died in one of the building's bathrooms. For many years after his death, strange things were reported to have taken place in that room, including the periodic flushing of the old-fashioned toilet. Plumbers were at a loss to explain the cause of the flushing, and the matter was merely added to the growing list of strange happenings associated with the house. When I mentioned this tale to Lucy, she indicated that she had not heard of any toilets flushing by themselves (the fixture in question had been replaced when the building was converted into an inn), but added that she had repeatedly heard water running in the upstairs bathrooms when she worked as a night clerk.

As I was about to leave, Lucy added one other curious detail. One night when she had nothing better to do, she began paging through the inn's guest book. As she was reading the comments guests had recorded, she came across one fascinating remark. Everything was fine, the note said, except that "the ghosts were noisy!"

Sure enough, the records showed that these guests had stayed in the very bedroom where Lucy felt so uncomfortable . . . and where the dollar bill had vanished and reappeared.

The door was locked from the inside . . .

June 22, 1992 As a history buff with a special interest in the California Gold Rush, I find every excuse I can to explore Highway 49 and the many mining camps and ghost towns that dot the Mother Lode. Today, after leaving a railroad show in Sacramento, I headed for the community of Auburn (where Highways 49 and 80 meet) and another run through the Gold Country.

Before turning south, I made a shopping stop in the old town section. Before long I found myself chatting with an Auburn old-timer who looked the part of a 49er himself. When the subject of ghosts came up, he told me that I should check with the bartender at a bar and restaurant down the street. Not wanting to pass up a ghost story, I made a beeline for the bar.

Upon venturing into the aged saloon, I felt as if I had walked back in time. The walls were covered with memorabilia, and several mounted critters of the Sierra Nevada appeared to stare at me as I surveyed the scene.

The bartender proved to be an affable chap who sported an outstanding handlebar mustache. When I mentioned ghosts, he nodded knowingly and began telling me about a fellow named George who once worked at the adjoining restaurant. Well along in years, George lived in a small shed behind the bar. The bartender didn't know how long George had lived there, or exactly when he died, but he did know that a bar or saloon had been housed in the building we were in since the early 1900s. The establishment had long been a popular gathering place for locals, and in the days before the back room was rearranged, old-timers frequently gathered around a large potbelly stove that was located there.

An eight-foot wall used to separate this back area from the bar itself. As the bartender described it, customers at the bar would hear the sounds of chairs being moved in the back room when the room was empty. It sounded as if someone was pushing them away from the stove or the nearby tables. Next, they would hear the rear door open and close. (The door had a bolt-like lock that could only be operated from within.) But, when the bartender or customers would hurry around the wall to see what was going on, invariably they found the room empty. And when they continued to the rear door, they saw that it was locked from the inside!

Activities such as these, combined with feelings of presence and assorted other sounds, caused locals to wonder whether George's spirit was frequenting the back room where men used to gather to drink and swap stories. In closing, however, the bartender indicated that things have been relatively quiet for the past few years. He added that the old potbelly stove and the wall dividing the two rooms were removed about eight years ago, and since then George's spirit has not been seen, heard, or felt.

The dead woman's likeness has frequently been seen . . .

June 22, 1992 Not far from Auburn, and with ghosts still on my mind, I stopped near Coloma, the site of the original gold discovery. There I visited the Sierra Nevada House, an aged two-story structure that houses a hotel, bar, and restaurant. Many years before, I had heard a ghost story about the building, and I decided to see whether anyone was around who could refresh my memory of the tale. Luckily for me, the lone couple at the bar were happy to recount the story to me.

Long ago, the couple explained, the building had been put on rollers and moved to its present site. (It was thought to have originally been located in a nearby area called Gold Hill.) Before it was moved, a young lady who worked in the restaurant found her boyfriend in an upstairs room with a prostitute. Enraged, the lady (whom I will call Julie) got into a spirited scrap with her boyfriend's companion. Soon the angry pair found themselves on the exterior balcony. Taking advantage of the setting, the prostitute ended the fray by throwing Julie over the railing. As it turned out, the fall not only ended the fight but Julie's life as well!

From that time on, strange things are said to have taken place in Room 4, where the fight began. Guests have reported such things as peculiar sounds emanating from the room and the movement of objects from place to place. Of even more interest, however, are the happenings associated with a huge mirror in the bar. As the story goes, the dead woman's likeness has frequently been seen in the mirror!

> *Author's Note:* History buffs may be interested to know that the mirror and its elaborate gold frame weigh over six hundred pounds. The mirror was transported to the Gold Country by ship and wagon, and is said to have traveled with the building when the structure was moved to its current location.

Vapors of steam rose from the boot . . .

July 26, 1992 In a roundabout way, this account got its start in the picturesque mining town of Johnsville. Located in the Feather River section of the Sierra Nevada, Johnsville is surrounded by the Plumas Eureka State Park. It boasts a colorful history, as well as the distinction of being the site where organized ski racing began in the Western Hemisphere.

It was in Johnsville that I met a park ranger who happened to mention the town of La Porte. This settlement boasts its own colorful history, not to mention a famous old Gold Country hotel. Spurred by this conversation, my wife and I decided to venture over the mountains to see what La Porte was like. ("Venture" is an apt word for this jaunt, which covered more than thirty miles, much of it over dirt roads.)

When we arrived, we stopped to enjoy a piece of pie and a cup of coffee in the dining room of the historic Union Hotel. When I asked our waiter about the background of the building, he brought up the subject of ghosts. I was unaware that a ghost story was part of the hotel's history, so naturally I was intrigued. After conferring with one of the restaurant's owners, the waiter brought me a written account.

According to this document, the tale goes something like this. In the late 1850s, with the cry of "Gold!" still echoing throughout the Mother Lode, an aged miner by the name of Frank Hudson teamed up with a younger man known as Adam Carson. Old-timers who knew them indicated that the pair differed in many respects besides age, including their work ethic and general outlook on life.

One dreary November morning while Adam slept—which seemed to be his habit when work needed to be done—Frank was hard at work in the mine. This day, however, proved to be different from all the rest, as Frank finally found the gold he had been seeking.

Racing from the mine, he roused Adam from his sleep and excitedly showed him an egg-sized nugget. Thrilled by the richness of the strike, the pair of miners decided to brave the snowstorm that had blown in and celebrate their good fortune at the Union Hotel in La Porte. Filling their saddlebags with chunks of gold, the twosome made their way to the mining town.

By the time they reached the hotel, they were weary and nearly frozen. Hauling their saddlebags into the building, they requested adjoining rooms ("the best in the house"), a couple of hot baths, and a bottle of whiskey.

After making their way to rooms 307 and 309, the two men wasted little time in stoking up the woodburning stoves in each room. Then they pulled off their snow-encrusted boots and clothing and headed for the baths down the hall. Here, with their saddlebags beside them and a bottle of whiskey within easy reach, they soaked in the tubs.

With a second bottle of whiskey following the first, and the heat from the tubs taking its toll, it was not long before the tired miners were good and drunk. Staggering back to their rooms, they were about to part for the evening when Adam opened his door and smelled leather burning. Rushing to the stove, he cussed luck as he discovered that he had placed his left boot too near the fire. When he held up the charred boot, his partner howled with laughter and told him not to worry because now that he was rich he could buy all the boots he wanted. With that, Frank went to his own room and collapsed on his bed in a drunken stupor.

Several hours later, Frank awoke to find a gag in his mouth and his arms and legs bound to the bed. Worse, the fire in the stove was out, and the windows were wide open, allowing the blizzard to blow snow into the room.

Unable to move or to cry out for help, Frank shivered from both fear and cold. Soon Adam entered the room. Standing over his partner, Adam smiled and told Frank that he was too trusting. Their partnership, he said, was over. "And since you won't be needing your boots any longer," he added, "I'm sure you won't mind giving me one of them." With that, he pulled off Frank's left boot to replace the one he had burned and stomped his foot into it. Hefting the saddlebags filled with gold, he bid Frank goodbye and left the room, taking care to lock the door behind him.

At the registration desk, Adam told the clerk that his buddy in room 309 was exhausted and was not to be disturbed for at least three days. Paying in advance for Frank's stay, Adam tipped the clerk handsomely and stalked out into the blizzard.

After three days, with neither Adam nor Frank having been seen, the clerk instructed the maid to service room 309. When she opened the door, the maid was appalled at the condition of the room. The windows were open, the room was icy cold, and snow covered the floor and furnishings. The maid promptly went to find the hotel manager and handyman to help her remove the snow.

As the men busied themselves shoveling snow from the floor, the maid began brushing it from the furniture. She was working on the bed when she suddenly gave a

31

scream and ran from the room. The bewildered men looked at the bed and immediately saw what had terrified her. In the process of brushing off the snow, she had uncovered the frozen face of Frank Hudson! The bulging eyes of the dead man seemed to stare at the open windows and the mountains beyond.

Although they were sickened by the sight, the manager and handyman proceeded to clear the snow off the rest of the body. Soon the sheriff was on the scene. After viewing the corpse, he decided to leave it where it lay until the next of kin (Hudson's sister in San Francisco) could be notified.

Unable to close the eyelids of the frozen miner, the sheriff placed two new pennies over the eyes in hopes of negating their look of terror. After sealing and locking the room, he swore out a warrant for the arrest of Adam Carson.

When Hudson's sister arrived a few days later, the sheriff and a helper accompanied her to room 309. Upon opening the door, the threesome were shocked to see that the room was perfectly clean and that there was no sign of a body! Thinking that he might have made a mistake, the sheriff hurriedly unlocked the adjoining room, where Adam Carson had stayed. When the door swung open, a terrific blast of icy air hit him. Yet, despite the cold, upon venturing inside the sheriff found a charred left boot on the bed with vapors of steam rising from it! When the sheriff picked up the boot, two shiny pennies fell to the floor.

To this day, legend states, Frank Hudson's body has not been found—and neither has Adam Carson or the stash of gold.

But the story doesn't end there, as over the years hotel guests have reported a number of strange happenings in room 309. One tale revolves around an aged miner who bedded down in the room around the turn of the century. According to his account, as he pulled off his trousers, a smattering of dirt fell from his cuffs and pockets. Glancing at the mess on the wood floor, he was surprised to see a pair of footprints in the dirt. Even more amazingly, the right foot was booted, while the left was bare! Other guests have told of intense feelings of cold in the room despite closed windows and a heater going full blast. In 1961 a gentleman reported awakening in the morning to a feeling of presence. Glancing around, he was surprised to find two shiny pennies on the pillow next to him!

My waiter had a number of other stories to tell as well (including one involving a disappearing wreath that he and others have experienced). With this background, I was more than happy to take him up on an offer to inspect room 309. With the manager's permission, we went up the stairs and into the unoccupied room. As I thought of the gruesome event that had reportedly taken place there, I must admit that I half-expected to feel the presence of Frank Hudson in the room, or at least some odd sensations. This, however, was not to be. Nor were there any footprints or shiny pennies to be seen.

Although the story of the two miners is a fascinating one, I confess that it has the earmarks of an imaginative legend. To cite just one mystery, if the dead miner and his greedy partner were the only players in this Gold Rush drama, how did the details of the story (such as the episode of the burned boot) come to be known? I suppose defenders of the story might say that Adam Carson did not necessarily die in the blizzard as he left town and that he could have confessed to his misdeed—and recounted all the details—during a drunken spree, or perhaps on his deathbed. And it may be that the other questions associated with the story have ready answers as well.

Perhaps it's best to let you decide for yourself whether such an event ever took place . . . or whether it is a colorful yarn invented by some long-ago storyteller that has made its way into the treasure chest of California lore.

Ghostly happenings at the Battery Point Lighthouse . . .

July 27, 1992 After leaving the Feather River country and the town of La Porte, my wife and I meandered through other areas of northern California before arriving at the north coast community of Crescent City. Along the way we stopped in Ferndale, just south of Eureka. Like Crescent City, Ferndale traces its history back to the 1850s. Among its many attractive features are several Victorian buildings. Unfortunately, as I write this, many of these venerable structures lean in a variety of directions as a result of the earthquake that rocked the area in April of this year. The town also boasts several accounts of ghostly happenings that I hope to learn more about at a later date.

From Ferndale we headed for the famed Samoa Cookhouse restaurant across the Samoa Bridge from Eureka. At least one restaurant employee has reported a ghostly presence on the second floor of this structure, an area that once served as a bunkhouse for workers at the adjoining lumberyard and mill. Although there is little to substantiate this particular account, it aroused my curiosity and perhaps is what prompted me to ask about ghosts when I visited the Crescent City history museum later in the day. My inquiry prompted one of the museum guides to call the curator of the nearby Battery Point Lighthouse, who resided there with her husband. Before I knew it, my wife and I were invited to visit this facility.

We were given a grand tour of the light station, which, like the town, hails from the 1850s. Our hostess, a delightful lady who was very knowledgeable about the place, had written a short history of the lighthouse and also documented several of the ghostly happenings reported to have taken place there. The information in this note is just a sample of the tales included in her account.

Among the manifestations reported at the lighthouse are the somewhat common occurrences of things being mysteriously moved, a rocking chair that rocks by itself (interestingly, the smell of pipe tobacco frequently fills the room while the chair is rocking), objects such as an antique glass chimney suddenly falling to the floor, feelings of presence accompanied by invisible hands being placed on people's sides, voices heard both inside and outside the building when no one is in the area, and the strange behavior of animals (in this case, cats) that seem to be reacting to "unseen things."

Another occurrence reminiscent of stories in countless other buildings is the sound of footsteps being heard when no one is about. At the lighthouse, these sounds are most often noticed during stormy weather. Sometimes the footsteps are heard on an hourly basis climbing the steps to the tower, as if the ghost of a past light keeper is checking the beacon to be sure it is still lit.

The account goes on to describe how a college group visited the lighthouse in the 1960s, bringing along ghost-detecting equipment. After a tour of the facility, they are said to have "scanned" three ghosts, including one who was the spirit of a child. No one knows who these spectral visitors might be, as there are no reports of anyone dying at the station. However, popular opinion seems to be that the two adult ghosts are those of Captain John Jeffrey, keeper of the light for nearly forty years, and Captain Samuel DeWolf of the ill-fated steamer *Brother Jonathan*. More than 150 people perished when the doomed steamer was lost on nearby St. George Reef in 1865. As for the child ghost, no one seems to know who it might be.

In closing this note, I would like to mention that a visit to Battery Point would be rewarding for anyone interested in lighthouses as well as for those who are curious about supernatural happenings. Visitors not only can get a feeling for what it is like to be a light keeper but can also purchase the packet that contains additional ghost stories associated with this historic place.

Author's Note: For more information about the Battery Point Lighthouse, and instructions on how to get there, contact the Del Norte County Historical Society, 577 H Street, Crescent City, California 95531. If you decide to visit, be sure to check the weather and tides beforehand, as they determine access to the lighthouse.

More mischief by Hattie Gragg? . . .

September 13, 1992 "What do you think of Hattie?" asked a waiter at one of my favorite Pacific Grove breakfast stops this morning. I knew that he was referring to Hattie Gragg, the supposed ghost at Monterey's Stokes Adobe (see "Hattie lives . . . ," page 20). As you might expect, his question proved to be the prelude to the waiter's own accounts of encounters with the mischievous spirit.

It seems that the waiter had worked at the aged adobe when it was a restaurant called The Old House. Along with a number of other workers, he had experienced several ghostly happenings while working in the establishment, such as feeling Hattie's presence and hearing her voice. Among other things, employees had also reported sighting Hattie's ghost near the main entrance, hearing sounds of a baby crying when no children were present, and feeling cold spots in various locations. In addition, there were reports of the appearance of a ghostly figure in Hattie's upstairs room as well as of objects being mysteriously moved.

Perhaps the most interesting event that my waiter experienced personally took place late one night after the restaurant had closed. That night, the waiter and a friend (who also worked there) were the last people to leave. As they approached the friend's car after locking up, they realized that some of the restaurant's lights had been turned back on. (This seems to be a favorite trick of the ghost, as other workers have reported similar happenings.) The weary twosome headed back to the building, unlocked the door, and turned off the lights again.

The pair were making ready to leave when suddenly a loud noise came from upstairs. As the waiter described it, there was a crash followed by the sounds of bottles rattling about, as if someone had dropped a box of bottles. Then came another noise, this time of a door being slammed. These sounds were doubly disconcerting, because not only was no one supposed to be in the building, but there were no doors in the area where the sounds seemed to come from!

Understandably spooked, my informant's companion turned around and ran for the car. The waiter, who depended on his friend for a ride home, had little choice but to follow—leaving the source of the sounds (not to mention the turning on of the lights) a complete mystery.

The fleeting figure disappeared from sight . . .

September 16, 1992 In addition to describing his own experiences at The Old House restaurant in the Stokes Adobe, the waiter in the previous note suggested that I talk to an acquaintance who had also worked there. This lead proved fruitful, as today I met this second man, a middle-aged gentleman who currently works as a waiter himself in a restaurant near Monterey's famed Fisherman's Wharf. Fortunately, things weren't too busy when I dropped by, and the waiter found time to share a few tales with me as he continued to cater to the customers at his two tables.

37

Interestingly, his first ghostly experience at The Old House took place before he was even hired. While he was sitting in the bar filling out an application form, he felt a definite presence, as if someone was watching him from the loft (a balcony section over the bar). Even though he was uncomfortable being scrutinized from above, he continued with his task, thinking that perhaps one of the owners was looking him over. Upon completing the form, he glanced up at the loft and saw the fleeting figure of an elderly woman disappear from sight.

This alone might not seem so strange (except that no one of that description should have been in the loft), but later the waiter experienced a second sighting of what might have been the spirit of Hattie Gragg. This incident occurred on the main staircase, where he saw the image of a small woman dressed in black. His description is said to match those of several other workers who said they had seen Hattie's ghost. Other than on the loft and the staircase, Hattie has reportedly been sighted in the front upstairs room (thought to have been her bedroom when she lived in the adobe), on the front balcony (which connects to the bedroom), and in front of the building. Some Old House workers, and even some passers-by, also claim to have seen a figure matching this description peeking from behind curtains in various rooms of the house.

The waiter also reported experiencing a non-Hattie-related incident described by many other people—hearing the sounds of a baby crying. As the waiter described them, the cries were soft and whimpering and almost seemed to come from between the walls.

In concluding, my informant had an even more dramatic episode to relate. Late one night, when he and one or two other people were in the building, they heard a loud crash upstairs, as if a china cabinet had fallen over. This was followed by the sounds of glass breaking. Unlike the people in the preceding note, the workers raced up the stairs to see what had happened. When they reached the second floor, all was secure . . . and not so much as a sliver of glass could be found on the floor!

> *Author's Note:* Stokes Adobe stories—and tales of Hattie Gragg—continue to multiply. I might mention that when the building was being renovated prior to the opening of The Old House restaurant, even the Monterey police got into the act. Several times they were called to the site to investigate such things as lights being turned on and off, unidentifiable sounds being heard, and items being moved. Naturally, no culprit was ever found.

The White Witch of Niles Canyon . . .

September 18, 1992 At ten o'clock this morning, I met a small television crew in the rear garden of the Robert Louis Stevenson House. They had come to Monterey from the Fremont area to shoot a film for educational television that would air prior to Halloween. They wanted to interview me for a segment about ghosts.

As might be expected, when the lady called to set up the interview, we got to talking about ghosts in her own area. It was she who told me about the "White Witch of Niles Canyon." She promised to jot the story down for me and bring it with her to Monterey. The following account is drawn from her notes as well as from conversations with her and one of the other crew members.

As the story goes, when the moon is full, motorists driving along Mill Creek Road (in the older parts of Niles Canyon) sometimes see the ghostly figure of a woman dressed in white. When an automobile approaches, she tries to hitch a ride. If the car does not stop, she attempts to grab onto it as it passes by. If it does stop, the apparition climbs in and makes herself comfortable in the passenger's seat . . . only to disappear as the car continues down the road! (I might mention that this is similar to stories that are told in various parts of the country, including a brief tale in my own *Ghost Notes* book.)

As for who the White Witch might be, legend states that she is the daughter of a long-dead landowner who lived in the area in the mid 1800s. Supposedly, one night she slipped out of her house to meet her lover. Hitching up a horse and buggy, she headed down the moonlit canyon. Somewhere along the way, the buggy became detached from the horse and tumbled down a rocky embankment. It landed in the creek at the bottom of the canyon, and the unfortunate young maiden drowned.

To this day, the story concludes, the lady's ghost continues to haunt Niles Canyon, perhaps still trying after all these years to reach her lover.

The swinging doors burst open . . .

May 14, 1993 While walking along Cannery Row, I stopped at one of the shops to visit an old friend who lives in the building that contains her store. This particular structure played a prominent role in John Steinbeck's *Cannery Row*. Naturally enough, our conversation turned to Steinbeck, his good friend Ed "Doc" Ricketts, and, of course, ghosts! I had already heard about several spooky incidents connected with the building, including some that had taken place in an art gallery that once occupied part of the structure. As I recorded in *Ghost Notes*, these happenings included the mysterious movement of a pair of saloon-style swinging doors that sometimes swung back and forth of their own accord. These doors were located near the rear of the gallery and separated the main portion from a small back room.

When I mentioned the swinging doors to my friend, she nodded and proceeded to tell me about her own experience with them. One afternoon, she related, she was visiting with the manager in the gallery. As three o'clock approached, the manager glanced at her watch and motioned for my friend to sit in a nearby chair. Choosing her own chair, the manager sat down. Holding up a newspaper as if she were reading it, she told my friend to watch the swinging doors.

Suddenly the doors burst open, as if someone had come barreling through them from the back room. Even though there was no one near them, the doors continued to swing violently back and forth. Seconds later, the pages of the manager's newspaper shook as if from a breeze created by someone walking by.

My awestruck friend naturally began to question the manager about these eerie happenings. Enjoying the moment, the manager only smiled and told her to be patient. Sure enough, some minutes later, the pages of the newspaper rustled once again, and the swinging doors banged open in the opposite direction!

In discussing these occurrences with the gallery's manager, my friend learned that the best guess of those in the know is that they are caused by the ghost of a man who had been a dishwasher in the building when part of it was a restaurant. Sadly, the dishwasher met an unhappy end, as his body was found on the railroad tracks behind the structure. His killer was never caught.

The eerie laugh became more and more demented . . .

May 16, 1993 I had a conversation today with a fellow I met several years ago, when he worked at the Highlands Inn resort hotel on the Big Sur coast. As we talked, he asked me about the haunted coal mine I had written about in *Incredible Ghosts of the Big Sur Coast*. As I related there, the Highlands coal mine was worked by

Chinese laborers in the 1880s. For an unknown reason—rumors had it that it was because of an outbreak of the plague, or because the mine owners were unable to meet the payroll—the mine foreman is said to have herded the workers into the mine and blasted it shut. Ever since, there have been reports of mournful cries and other strange happenings in the vicinity of the mine.

It turned out that this former Highlands worker had a story of his own about the site. When he was working at the luxurious resort, he told me, he and a buddy once hiked to the mine site to see what they could see. While there, they began hearing eerie, humanlike laughing sounds that seemed to come from the trees. As the sounds became louder—sounding more and more like they were coming from a man with a high-pitched voice—the two men looked around, but could find nothing out of the ordinary. By then my friend's buddy (a macho-type individual who stood over six feet tall and weighed about 250 pounds) was so spooked that he took off on the run!

Feeling scared himself, but suspecting a prank, my friend bravely took another look around. Although there was no one to be seen, the sounds grew louder still, and the eerie laugh became more and more demented. Finally, my friend couldn't stand it any longer and decided to join his buddy in hightailing it out of the area!

"Spirited" goings-on at the Hotel Willow . . .

May 29, 1993 During a visit to the historic Gold Country settlement of Jamestown—which, by the way, is a "must" stop for anyone interested in the period of the argonauts—I got to talking with the night manager of the beautifully restored Jamestown Hotel. In response to my question about ghosts that are said to haunt one of the former mining community's old hotels, she smiled and said that even though the Jamestown itself might not be the establishment I was looking for, a number of strange things had taken place there. Among them were feelings of presence, unidentifiable sounds, and toilets flushing in empty bathrooms. Nevertheless, she indicated that the place I was seeking was probably the Hotel Willow.

After getting directions, my wife and I enjoyed a pleasant stroll along the main street of town to the Willow. There, after inquiring about ghosts, we were introduced to a delightful woman who was helping in the kitchen. This lady, whom I will call Anne, had worked at the facility for more than fifteen years, and for the last five years she had been seriously researching its history. Having accumulated more than a thousand pages of notes, interviews, articles, anecdotes, and oral accounts, she probably knew more about the place than any other living person.

Among Anne's records were tales of strange and memorable occurrences dating back to the hotel's earliest days (it was built in the 1860s). These happenings included several unnatural deaths involving people of all ages, with both murder and suicide being among the causes. She also informed us about a number of other "unnatural" phenomena, mentioning saloon doors that swung back and forth by themselves, warm feelings of presence experienced by people in different parts of the building, toilets flushing of their own accord, and lights that turned off and on for no apparent reason. (On one occasion when the structure's electricity had been shut off, one of the aged electric lights turned on by itself . . . only to turn *off* when the power was restored!)

Anne also touched on other, even more eerie incidents. She described, for example, how likenesses of individuals appeared in photographs (both color and black and white) when no such people were present. She also told of sightings of ghostly figures in the barroom and in other parts of the hotel. Apparently, the figure observed most often was that of a man about five feet, seven inches tall who was usually dressed in miner's clothing, although taller men in more formal attire were also observed.

By this time Anne had to return to work, so we ended our conversation with plans to meet again. She promised that on this later occasion she would let me peruse the documents that she had collected as well as read her own writings. So, with luck this account will be continued, and somewhere along the way we'll learn more about the "spirited" goings-on at the Hotel Willow.

> *Author's Note:* For a follow-up to this account, see "More on the Hotel Willow . . . ," page 47.

Ghostly guests at the Hotel Jeffery . . .

June 18, 1993 Research for my children's book *Tales and Treasures of the California's Gold Rush* has brought my wife and me back to the Gold Country. While winding our way along Highway 49, we stopped at several of the old boom towns and mining camps. At each stop we sought out old-timers and hunted for information on lost Gold Rush treasures, stagecoach robberies, and the like.

One of our first stops was at the Chamber of Commerce office in the tiny town of Coulterville. There we met a delightful lady whose family had settled in Coulterville in the mid 1800s. Unfortunately for my children's book, she had no information to impart about lost treasures and long-ago bandits. But when I mentioned ghosts, she looked at me in surprise and said, "It's funny you ask!" Picking up a folder that was on her desk, she handed it to me. Printed on the cover was the word "Ghosts." While I quickly skimmed its half-dozen or so handwritten pages, she told me that the manager of the Hotel Jeffery—the largest and most imposing building in town—had given her the folder just the day before.

A quick phone call later, our new acquaintance had secured permission for us to copy the folder's contents, as well as an invitation to visit with the Jeffery's manager. As it turned out, the manager was a friend of the woman we had met at the Hotel Willow in Jamestown, whom I have called Anne (as related in "'Spirited' goings-on at the Hotel Willow . . . ," page 42). In fact, it was at Anne's urging that the information in the "Ghosts" folder had been recorded. We were planning to visit Anne again that very evening, and I would learn then that she was very familiar with the Hotel Jeffery. Not only had she worked at the hotel catering parties and the like, but she had talked to several people who had experienced strange things there. On one occasion, she had even walked through the building with a psychic.

The manager, meanwhile, provided us with additional information about the Hotel Jeffery. We learned that the inn dates back to at least 1851 (some sources suggest its history goes back even further). Other than catering to miners, it was a favorite overnight stagecoach stop for people going to and from Yosemite. Names on its register range from presidents and royalty to gangsters and gunslingers. Now restored and refurbished, the hotel is still well known to travelers to the Gold Country, and it continues to cater to people from all walks of life. Its Magnolia Saloon remains a popular gathering place and is said to be "the oldest bar in California."

If we can believe the stories, the Jeffery may even cater to some who have long since passed on. According to stories that have been handed down, as well as aged newspaper accounts, a number of ghostly guests have been sighted in various parts of the structure. Appropriately, the ghost that is most often observed in the saloon is that of a miner. The restaurant, on the other hand, seems to cater more to ghosts of the female variety. One such entity—thought to be the ghost of a maid who worked at the facility in the early 1900s—delights in rearranging silverware after tables have been set. In particular, knives are mysteriously moved from their customary spots and placed horizontally above the place settings. Other dining-room incidents occur in the dead of night, when objects are turned upside down. Finally, the ghostly figure of a female guest has been observed both in the restaurant and on the hotel's second floor. (Incidentally, the maid who rearranges the silverware is also said to frequent the hotel. Usually her image is spotted on the staircase leading to the second floor. If you happen to visit the Jeffery, check the fourth or fifth step from the top.)

Another sighting of a lady ghost took place in room 10. One night when a couple occupied the room, the husband was awakened by the sound of the door closing. Watching from the bed, he saw the ghostly figure of a woman dressed in a long, old-fashioned gown. Approaching the room's rocking chair, the apparition sat and silently rocked for several minutes. After the image disappeared, the startled husband woke his wife, wondering aloud if he had been dreaming. Climbing from the bed, he approached the rocking chair and felt the seat. To his surprise, it felt warm, as if someone had been sitting on it! As for his wife, although she didn't see the spirit, she did feel its presence.

Room 22 also boasts some ethereal guests. Apparently the spirits of both a man and a woman frequent this room. The man is said to be in his fifties. He sports a beard and is on the tall, thin side. The woman appears to be quite a bit younger, perhaps in her thirties. Some seem to think that it is these ghosts who visit the dining room during the night and turn things upside down.

Other incidents associated with room 22 took place when the building was being renovated. Probably the best known of these events involved some carpenter's tools and building materials that had been left in the room overnight. On more than one occasion, when workers showed up for work in the morning, they found the items strewn about the hall.

In reference to the psychic's walk through the building (as witnessed by Anne), several interesting incidents were recorded. Unfamiliar with the structure, and knowing little of its history, the psychic wandered from room to room describing things she felt and saw. Included in her remarks were the names and descriptions of various people who had stayed in the rooms. At times she also commented on their personalities and some of their experiences (both before and during their stay in the hotel). It is said that a surprising number of the psychic's findings that were traceable through hotel records and such proved to be accurate. So perhaps there is more to experience at the Jeffery than charming rooms and excellent meals! (Incidentally, a parapsychologist who works with the Los Angeles Police Department has said that the ghosts at the Jeffery "are friendly and mean no harm.")

More on the Hotel Willow . . .

June 18, 1993 From Coulterville to Jamestown is a pleasant drive of less than twenty-five miles. In Jamestown, my wife and I had our reunion with Anne, our source for information about the Hotel Willow (see "'Spirited' goings-on at the Hotel Willow . . . ," page 42). True to her word, Anne brought with her a collection of documents concerning the historic hotel.

Historic it certainly is! The original building was constructed in 1862, and some sources indicate that the Willow may be the oldest surviving commercial wooden structure in the Mother Lode. Originally it was a multistoried structure, but due to a series of fires the facility now has just one story. Interestingly, in looking through the stack of material Anne brought to our meeting, I found that at least one ghost expert has expressed the opinion that some of the fires may have been supernaturally set. This conclusion stems from a conflagration that dates back to the 1890s. Apparently, lacking water to fight the flames that threatened the town, local residents used dynamite to bring the fire under control. One of the few landmark buildings to survive was the Willow. One source, however, tells this tale differently, stating that "most of the town was blown up to save the Willow!" Maybe it is this last remark that prompted the psychic researcher to suggest that perhaps the ghosts of the townspeople who were killed in the holocaust resent the fact that the Willow survived and are in some way responsible for the subsequent fires.

Other accounts point to additional troubled spirits that may also have played a part in the fires. Among them are the ghosts of between twenty and thirty miners who were reportedly killed when a mine shaft caved in before the Willow was built on the site. (A second source indicates that the deaths were caused by an explosion in the mine.) This information is doubly interesting because one of the many Willow-related ghost stories suggests that a "grudge-bearing, bald-headed, pajama-clad spirit" that has been seen on the premises may be responsible for both the mine accident and the fires as well.

Various other tragic events are associated with the Willow or its site. Among the stories are the supposed violent deaths of at least three people in the saloon. The same source also mentions the long-ago death of a guest who was strung up in his room by a lynch mob!

Speaking of lynchings, before a fire destroyed the hotel portion of the structure in the 1970s, one of its rooms earned fame (or infamy) as a "hanging room." The hanging room was a small upstairs guest room that was located in the back of the hotel. It is described as dark and "spooky" with peeling wallpaper and a "weird little window" that faced the hallway. Among the most interesting of the tales connected with this room is one that dates back to the 1800s. It tells of two men—who were unknown to each other—hanging themselves in the room on succeeding nights! Another note states that one of the devastating 1970s fires started in the hanging room when it was empty. If this coincidence isn't enough to give one pause, consider the fact that "dark figures" were allegedly seen "flitting among the flames."

Other than fires, one of the best known of the tragic events connected with the Willow involves one of the hotel's former owners, who apparently killed his wife in the hotel before turning the gun on himself. Various rumors circulate about this incident, and the owner may have taken the real story to the grave with him.

To return to the subject of ghosts, apart from the bald-headed man I have already mentioned, another spirit who has been sighted at the hotel is a "frizzy" redheaded woman who was supposedly murdered by her husband in the bar. A small and "furtive" man is also sometimes seen wandering about the establishment, as if he is looking for someone, or something. Then there's the chap who looks like a gambler and sports a dashing mustache and a spotless black suit. On more than one occasion this dapper gentleman is said to have appeared at the bar, only to disappear when he is served.

With several accounts having been written about the Willow, it is probably safe to assume that *something* strange is going on. If we can believe a psychic investigator who exorcised the building in the late 1970s, there are still spirits that frequent the facility. Fortunately, this investigator thinks that he was able to rid the structure of some of its ghosts during the first of two séances he conducted. These spirits included a foul-mouthed, loud-talking woman who had stayed at the hotel in the 1950s; a former worker at the facility who felt he had been wrongly accused of stealing; and an older woman who is thought to have died when her own home burned. The investigator, however, goes on to say that other spirits continue to linger in the building. Two are said to be miners who are thought to have worked the mine that once ran under the Willow, while two others are women.

Before closing this account, I should add that even though the establishment is still known as the Hotel Willow, today there are no rooms to let. However, if you are looking for excellent meals and an authentic Gold Country bar, the Willow is an excellent choice. True, things "of a supernatural nature" continue to be reported . . . but these happenings are not negative, and perhaps they only add to the atmosphere. As a past dining-room manager stated, "The ghosts don't bother the customers!"

Mysterious happenings in Mokelumne Hill . . .

June 19, 1993 The morning after our meeting with Anne in Jamestown, my wife and I continued north on Highway 49, passing through such places as Sonora (which also boasts several ghosts) and Angels Camp (of Jumping Frog fame). We soon found ourselves in Mokelumne Hill, or Mok Hill, as it is known to the locals. A right turn into the old section of the town brought us to the Hotel Leger. Built in 1852, this two-story structure was first known as Hotel de L' Europe, Hotel de France, or the Grand Hotel (take your pick, as sources differ). After a damaging fire (thought to have been in the 1870s), George Leger, who originally built the establishment, restored the structure. Upon reopening it, he named it after himself.

During our stop at the hotel, the owners (a husband and wife team) took turns in relating a few of the mysterious happenings that have been reported there in recent years. One such event occurred on a Saturday morning in

October of 1992, when a man who was staying at the facility rose early and was taking a look around. While he was in the theater—in reality Mokelumne Hill's original courthouse, which was built in the early 1850s and now serves as part of the hotel—he experienced the ghostly presence of a lady. In communicating with her he learned that her name was Elizabeth and that she was a prostitute. Supposedly she had turned to prostitution during the town's "heyday" to support a young boy who was in her care (possibly her son).

As a follow-up to this account, in February of 1993 a man who was staying in room 2 mentioned that he was awakened in the middle of the night by a female form. More curious than frightened, the man was able to learn that the apparition's name was . . . Elizabeth (or Liz for short). Now, if you are like me, you can't help but wonder if the two Elizabeths are (or were) the same person (or spirit) . . . and, if so, what she was doing in room 2. But before we jump to any conclusions, I must mention that in the 1870s a woman is said to have died in a fire in that room. So, before we think unjust thoughts about our ghostly friend, maybe we should entertain the possibility that the spirit in room 2 is that of the woman who lost her life there. On the other hand, the same source goes on to say that a young boy died in room 3 during the same fire. Inasmuch as the prostitute in the theater had a young boy in her care, maybe the two Elizabeths really are one after all!

Leaving this mystery for you to ponder, I will move on to an account about George Leger. Apparently he was quite a ladies' man, and, if we can believe some of the things that have been written about him, his death was at least partly due to his romantic involvement with the girlfriend of one of his male friends. To complicate matters, the friend not only was disgruntled over the competition for the lady but also owed Leger money. According to rumors of the day, the jealous lover hired a "hit man" to kill Leger, with the idea of ridding himself of both his debt and his competitor.

As the story goes, the assassin waited for Leger in the hallway of his hotel and shot him as he left his room (number 7). The commotion roused hotel workers and friends of Leger, who carried the gravely wounded man into his room, where he died. The killer, meanwhile, escaped during the confusion.

The long-range results of Leger's death are a number of ghostly happenings that are attributed to his spirit. Interestingly, not only does Leger's spirit lurk about the premises, but according to an account about the aged building, the ghost of the man who hired his assassin is said to accompany Leger in some of his adventurous pursuits. Thus, the two apparitions are thought to haunt the hotel together, and supposedly have been observed chasing ladies from room to room!

Perhaps on a more believable note, a relatively recent happening involving the ghost of George Leger took place in the late 1980s. On this occasion, two children (aged ten and twelve) rushed out of one of the hotel's rooms and told their father, who was involved in the building's restoration, that someone had told them to "be quiet!" After the father looked around and found nothing, the children reluctantly returned to the room. However, later that day the threesome had occasion to visit George Leger's old room, where they saw a picture of the hotel's founder on the wall. "That's the man who told us to be quiet!" the children exclaimed. Not knowing what to make of the situation, the father could do little more than shake his head in bewilderment.

As with several other old hotels (both in and out of the Gold Country), the longer you're about the more ghost stories seem to surface. Among the additional Hotel Leger accounts I uncovered were those involving the sounds of a woman wailing that are heard in the theater, strange humanlike shadows that come and go (especially in room 7), banquet sounds that come from the hotel when it is empty, pictures that fall from the walls for no apparent reason, room doors that lock from within when no one is in the rooms, and a dog that was found on a roof when there was no way for it to get there. Perhaps, as with the Hotel Willow, these tales only add to the charm of the place. Certainly my wife and I found the establishment most inviting. And if you enjoy seafood, you should know that the hotel's Friday night calamari feeds can't be beat!

The darker side of Mission San Miguel . . .

July 2, 1993 While traveling to San Luis Obispo for research purposes, my wife and I stopped at Mission San Miguel, approximately thirty-five miles to the north. Unless you are familiar with the mission's history, it may come as a surprise that many ghost buffs are of the opinion that San Miguel, perhaps more than any other California mission, is a prime candidate for haunted happenings. Their reasoning stems from an event that occurred there during the California Gold Rush, long after the padres had left and the mission had ceased serving as a church.

Briefly, the tale goes something like this. In 1848, when the William Reed family operated an inn and a general store at the site, a small party of men met at the establishment. The visitors are said to have been two drifters from the Mother Lode and three deserters from a man-of-war anchored in Monterey Bay. Upon staying the night they became friendly with Mr. Reed, a talkative sort who liked to boast about his success in the mines. Thinking that Reed might have stashed his treasure somewhere about the place, the five men secretly made plans to return the next night and search for his wealth.

53

As morning dawned, the men casually bid their host goodbye, saddled their mounts, and left the inn. However, instead of leaving the area they traveled only a short distance. Soon they pulled off the main trail and waited for darkness.

What happened next has been debated in numerous texts, with many agreeing that the five men returned to the inn late that night. In their frenzy to find the hidden gold, they cruelly murdered everyone they found, including the entire Reed family. Although the killers got away (empty-handed, I might add), they were soon caught, and, they too, met untimely ends.

With this background, you can see why those with an interest in the supernatural are not surprised when ghostly tales are told about the aged mission and its grounds. Among the happenings that have been reported is the appearance of a bloody handprint on a wall that could not be washed off. The wall was even painted to blot out the print, but years later it was still visible. Reportedly, the bloody print could only be seen by certain people, and then only late at night. This prompted some to wonder whether the mark appeared at the time of night that the Reed murders took place.

Another sighting resembles a white spectre that appears to glide about the grounds. While some pooh-pooh this account, the fact that the apparition has been mentioned in more than one source makes others think twice about its authenticity.

Today San Miguel is once again under the jurisdiction of the Catholic Church, and some of the Franciscan brothers who have been headquartered there are said to have recorded a number of odd happenings. One source tells of accounts of water pumps that work by themselves and machinery (or tools) moving of their own accord. There are descriptions of the air in the old wing becoming "almost electric" as well as stories of objects in that wing being moved mysteriously, including items that for unknown reasons have been found in rooms where they haven't been for more than one hundred years.

Other reports reflect the belief that the ghost of William Reed haunts the facility, walking the halls in a belated attempt to protect his family and home. Legends even hint that Reed himself is the source of the bloody handprint on the wall.

More up-to-date stories tell of psychics who have visited the grounds and who report that "there is something there." These accounts say that spirits of the dead continue to dwell at the complex and that they are still trying to protect their home.

Given the darker side of the history of Mission San Miguel, you can appreciate why I stopped by to ask an acquaintance who worked there about anything new in the way of ghostly happenings. At first my contact indicated that things have been quiet as far as ghosts are concerned. However, after thinking for a moment, she went on to say that she had recently talked to a young married couple who had toured the mission. In discussing the various rooms they had visited, the wife inquired about one of the bedrooms. Somewhat self-consciously, she related that for some reason she was overcome by a "feeling of fear" when she entered the room. Interestingly, and unbeknownst to her, the room in question was where some of the killings had taken place.

With this short tale jogging her memory, my friend went on to say that a similar experience had also taken place rather recently. This incident involved a girl of about ten who, with her mother, had ventured into one of the rooms where victims' bodies had been found. As with the preceding account, upon entering the room the girl was overwhelmed by "feelings of fear" . . . even though neither she nor her mother were aware of the killings that had taken place at the mission.

The apparition had no face . . .

July 3, 1993 After spending the night in San Luis Obispo, my wife and I stopped by a pastry shop in the heart of the city for an early morning cup of coffee. While we were there, we got to talking to the lady in charge, who had lived in the area for many years and was quite knowledgeable about the town. When I asked about ghosts, her eyes lit up, and she began telling us about various buildings in and about the city that were said to be haunted. With her stories stirring our imaginations, we decided to try to document some of the tales she had told.

Among our first stops was the San Luis Obispo Public Library. As it turned out we spent much of the day there poring over microfilm copies of old newspapers. Among the several mentions of ghosts we found was one that is an appropriate follow-up to the tales about San Miguel, for it also involves a mission ghost . . . this time one that was encountered in the garden of the mission of San Luis Obispo.

This tale dates back to the early years of the church, sometime between the mission's founding in 1772 and 1800. During an Indian uprising, a monk—as well as several people who had taken refuge at the church—are said to have been killed. After the uprising was over and things slowly returned to normal, another friar was assigned to San Luis Obispo. During harvest time at the church, which was also about the time of All Souls Day, the new padre took to walking in the garden at night to say his prayers. It was during one of these walks that he saw the ghostly figure of a man dressed in a robe and cowl. As he approached the apparition, it vanished from sight.

Being both curious and concerned, the young friar was determined to learn more about the mysterious figure. With this in mind, on a second night—when the full moon lit up the garden—he hid behind a pillar and watched. Soon he saw the cloaked figure strolling through the garden with his hands folded into the sleeves of his robe. Rosary beads were dangling from the sleeve openings, as if the ghostly monk had the cross clasped in his hands. As the figure approached, the young friar attempted to talk to it. Instead of receiving an answer, he experienced an icy feeling.

The young priest, however, was not to be denied. Summoning all of his courage, he reached out and pulled the cowl from the ghost's head . . . only to discover that the apparition had no face! Unnerved by this frightening experience, he dropped to his knees in prayer. After regaining his composure, he raised his head and looked about the garden. The mysterious figure was gone. The source that reported this story did not explicitly say that the garden ghost was the spirit of the monk who had been killed in the Indian uprising . . . but it did state that thereafter the young friar chose not to venture into the garden when the moon was full because he wanted "the ghost of 'the monk' to rest in peace."

The presence materialized into an old woman . . .

September 4, 1993 While on my daily walk, I stopped by a friend's photography studio in Pacific Grove, where I had a chance meeting with a local couple I met several years ago. As they knew my interest in ghosts, the conversation soon got around to their experiences in a Monterey house they used to live in, which was located near the Royal Presidio Chapel.

One incident that I found particularly interesting was related (for the most part) by the wife, whom I will call Jane. It seems that the couple's bedroom was on the second floor, while the only bathroom was at ground level. On several occasions when Jane made a nighttime trek to the bathroom, she passed a spot on the stairs that was colder than any other part of the house. It also had a "feeling of presence" about it. More asleep than awake when she made these bathroom jaunts, Jane never gave the cold spot or the feeling of presence much thought.

That is, she never thought seriously about them until one night when she heard a noise downstairs. Being familiar with the house, she normally made her way in the dark without putting on her glasses. This time, however, thinking that someone might be in the house, she put on her glasses and bravely started down the stairs. Upon reaching the cold spot, she made an abrupt stop . . . as the presence she had so often felt suddenly materialized into the form of a kindly old woman! With the figure radiating a feeling of warmth and protection, Jane soon regained her composure and continued down the stairs. With newfound courage she proceeded to search the house, feeling that she was being watched over and protected by the ghostly presence.

Because of this and other experiences, both Jane and her husband were convinced that the house was haunted. They also believed that a loving and caring spirit was watching over them. However, the significance of the sighting didn't fully hit them until sometime later, when they answered a knock at the door to find two ladies standing on their front porch. One of the visitors explained that she had lived in the house when she was young and was wondering whether she could show her friend the inside. After being invited in, the ladies wandered through the house in the company of Jane and her husband. As they toured the building, the former resident talked about some of her memories of incidents that had taken place there.

One of these memories was of a tragic event involving one of her aunts. Sadly, the aunt had become depressed while staying in the house and had committed suicide in the garage. Upon hearing this, Jane asked what the aunt had looked like. As you have probably guessed, the description of the dead woman matched the figure that Jane had seen on the stairs!

Although this resemblance might seem to be nothing more than coincidental, Jane's visitor was able to impart another detail that gave new significance to the sighting. Evidently, her aunt had written a note before she died. After expressing sorrow and apologies, the note had gone on to say that she would return to the house and watch over those who were there!

Author's Note: As it turned out, Jane and her husband are not the only people who believe that the house in question is haunted. I was later able to verify that their former residence was a building I had already written about in the very last entry of my original *Ghost Notes* book (dated June 15, 1990). My source on that occasion was a lady who had also lived in the old house. She had described how a number of people had experienced a variety of weird occurrences, including hearing the sounds of footsteps going up the stairs, followed by doors being opened and closed. The sounds left the impression that someone was crossing the upstairs landing and going into a room. Interestingly, this source had done some further checking and discovered that a suicide had once taken place on the property—and that the room at the end of the upstairs landing had been the victim's bedroom.

A talking ghost . . .

January 14, 1994 An interesting coincidence occurred yesterday as I was preparing for a talk at Pacific Grove's Asilomar Conference Grounds. I was planning to tell several Robert Louis Stevenson House ghost stories in honor of the 100th anniversary of the writer's death. Little did I know that I would soon have another tale to add to the collection!

As I was working, I received a telephone call from a woman in southern California who had purchased a copy of *Ghost Notes* during a visit to Monterey. Of special interest to her were the accounts about the Stevenson House, as they reminded her of a strange experience her mother, whom I will call Louise, had there in 1971.

The caller explained that Louise and her husband were taking a guided tour of the building with a group of other visitors. One of their stops was at the entrance of the children's nursery at the end of the upstairs hall. Like the other rooms in the aged adobe, the nursery contained antique objects and furnishings. Louise was particularly fascinated by the old toys that were scattered about the room. Her fascination with the toys stemmed from her childhood, as when she was young she had played with similar toys that had belonged to her grandparents and great-grandparents.

With a flood of memories coming back to her as she peered into the room, Louise lingered at the nursery's entrance as the rest of the party continued the tour. After a time she realized that she was the only one still there. As she was about to leave, she glanced down the hall in the opposite direction from which the tour had gone. There she saw a second guide dressed in an old-fashioned, Spanish-style costume coming toward her. As the guide approached, Louise commented on the toys, only to have the guide answer in Spanish. Unable to understand her, Louise nodded her thanks and hurried after the tour.

Soon after Louise caught up with her group in the rear gardens, the tour broke up. As she and her husband were about to leave, the tour guide asked Louise what she thought of the house. She responded that she had particularly enjoyed the nursery, but that she had had a hard time understanding the other guide. Upon hearing this, the first guide looked puzzled and said emphatically, "But there *isn't* another guide!" To add to the mystery, she went on to say that no one else could have been in the building, because when tours were in progress all the outside doors were locked, preventing anyone from entering the house!

Finding this account of considerable interest, today I decided to follow my caller's advice and telephone her mother in Texas to verify the information. Not only did Louise confirm the story, but she added some intriguing details. Among them was the fact that prior to her visit to the Stevenson House, she had been unaware of any ghost stories connected with the building. She also gave a description of the mysterious guide, saying that she appeared to be in her thirties or forties and was of medium height. The guide wore a dark, old-fashioned, Spanish-style costume, and spoke formally in Spanish. Perhaps most interesting of all, Louise told me that upon leaving the upstairs hall she glanced back toward the guide . . . only to realize that she had disappeared!

It is incidents like these—receiving unsolicited stories from people I have never met and who have nothing to gain from sharing their tales—that make me continue to believe that there are things going on that we don't understand. Louise's experience is especially interesting, as it enables us to add another dimension to the many ghostly tales that are connected with Monterey's Robert Louis Stevenson House . . . a talking ghost!

"Somebody should do something for the lady in the next room . . ."

January 31, 1994 While I was enjoying a cup of coffee at a delightful French bakery in Monterey, a docent from Big Sur's Point Sur Lighthouse stopped by my table and started talking about my *Ghost Notes* book and its accounts about the lightkeeper's house. Located about twenty-two miles south of Carmel, the Point Sur Lighthouse was established in 1889. Its setting is one of the most spectacular on the California coast. Perched atop a gigantic rock that juts out of the ocean, the facility commands a breathtaking view of Big Sur's rugged shore. Besides the lighthouse, there are several other buildings on the rock. The largest of these structures is built of stone and housed the lightkeepers and their families. It was in this aged dwelling that the ghostly happenings are said to have taken place.

As I related in *Ghost Notes*, it was in a bedroom on the third floor of this building that a teenage girl died of consumption (tuberculosis) around the turn of the century. Toward the end the unfortunate young lady was overcome with fits of coughing. Long after her death, the sounds of her coughing continued to be heard in the room by both visitors and residents of the house.

My new acquaintance was able to add a couple of tales that contribute to the credibility of these accounts. The first concerns an eight-year-old boy, the son of a past lightkeeper, who slept in the room next to the one in which the teenage girl had died. Even though he was unfamiliar with the stories about the house, on more than one occasion he came downstairs complaining that he couldn't sleep because a girl (or woman) was coughing in the room next to him. As you might expect, the room in question was empty.

The second story described an event that took place several years later, when the lightkeeper's house was being re-roofed. While the work was in progress, one of the roofers spent a night at the house, staying in what had been the eight-year-old boy's room. Upon going down to breakfast the next morning, he remarked, "If it isn't already too late, somebody should do something for the lady in the next room, because she has a terrible cough!" Needless to say, he was unaware that there was no one in the room at the time.

A Hearst Castle haunting . . .

February 12, 1994 Like many people, over the years I have become fascinated by the William Randolph Hearst Castle in San Luis Obispo County. Certainly, anyone who visits this coastal landmark can't help but be awed by it. Not only are its buildings and furnishings unique, but the vast acreage that made up the original grounds of William R. Hearst's "country home" helped to enhance its magnificent setting.

While doing research for two past publications, I became familiar with selected sections of the Hearst Ranch holdings and several stories of strange and unexplained happenings associated with them. However, even though the accounts were remotely connected with Hearst Castle, it wasn't until today that I heard a firsthand report of a ghost at the estate.

The story really began yesterday, when a young teacher stopped by our booth at the teachers' conference we are attending in Oakland. As she seemed to be interested in my books on ghosts, I told her about some of the stories I have collected since *Ghost Notes* was published. After our talk she thanked me for sharing these tales and went on her way.

Today the young lady, whom I will call Bonnie, returned to the booth, obviously wanting to talk. After a few minutes of friendly chat, she mentioned, somewhat self-consciously, that when she was twelve she had had a ghostly experience at Hearst Castle. With this as an opener, she began to tell me about her family's visit to the estate. However, when she got to the part about the ghost, she blushed, began to get teary-eyed, and changed the subject. Within a few minutes she had regained her composure and again began telling me about the incident.

As Bonnie described it, everything about the Hearst Castle visit was fine until her family and the rest of the tour group entered the master bedroom. It was in this room that she saw the ghostly figure of an older woman in the large bed. As the group continued to filter into the room, the lady, who appeared to have been sleeping, sat up in the bed and looked at the people. Upon spotting Bonnie, she smiled and indicated that she wanted her to come closer. Knowing that the bed was off-limits (as visitors are allowed only in certain parts of the rooms), and not knowing who the lady was, Bonnie chose to stay with her family and the rest of the group. However, all the while they were in the room she stared at the woman, who continued to smile and beckon to her to come nearer.

When the tour leader finished talking about the bedroom and its priceless furnishings, the group followed him to the next stop. As soon as they left the bedroom, Bonnie asked her father if he had seen the lady. As it turned out, neither he nor anyone else in her family had seen the spirit.

To this day Bonnie is bothered by the sighting. She not only wonders who the lady was, but why she was visible only to her, and why she gestured to her to come closer. In listening to her account, and observing how emotional she became when she told me the tale, I was touched by her sincerity and believe that I am one of only a few people with whom she has shared her experience.

Author's Note: The other stories connected with the vast Hearst land holdings that I have reported in my previous books include an account of the Santa Lucia Mountains' "Ghost of Gold" mine (in *Incredible Ghosts of the Big Sur Coast*) and a number of stories associated with Mission San Antonio and its surrounding territory (in *Ghostly Tales and Mysterious Happenings of Old Monterey*). Although located in southern Monterey County, the areas in question were either near, or part of, the original Hearst property.

More happenings at the old Hotel Del Monte . . .

February 16, 1994 Yesterday I received a couple of phone calls that eventually led to more tales of strange goings-on at the Naval Postgraduate School in Monterey (formerly the Hotel Del Monte). One was from an administrator at the school, and the other was from a lady who had contacted me several months ago about where she could obtain pictures of the old hotel.

It was the administrator who arranged for me to meet this evening with a young woman who had been staying in room 211 of Herrmann Hall (the main section of the old hotel) with her husband and 14-month-old child. (It turned out that my other caller had also spoken with this lady and knew that the family had a story to tell.) In addition to the woman and her toddler (whom I will refer to as Polly and Paul), we were joined by the administrator's assistant. Later in the meeting, a person from the admiral's office also joined our gathering. I had my trusty tape recorder with me, and these notes are compiled in part from the resulting recording.

The administrator had already told me quite a bit about Polly's experiences, but as we chatted Polly added a number of details. It seems that when Polly first entered Herrmann Hall a few nights ago, she felt a presence—or at least a strangeness—about the facility. Although she knew nothing of the ghost stories connected with the building, she half-jokingly remarked to her husband, "This place is haunted!" Only once before had she felt this way—upon entering a hotel in Colorado where she and her husband went to stay before their baby was born. On that occasion, Polly was so uncomfortable as they checked in that she refused to stay at the hotel, and the couple ended up taking lodgings elsewhere.

Despite her strange feeling about Herrmann Hall, Polly and her family proceeded to try to make themselves comfortable in room 211. As soon as she entered the room, however, Polly felt an intense cold. Apparently little Paul also felt something, as he was happy and content until the moment they walked into the room. Immediately he began fussing and pointing to the door, indicating that he wanted to go back into the hall. He also seemed to see some presence in the room, and tried to talk to it in his infant's babble. In order to quiet him and avoid disturbing the other guests, Polly carried him back into the hall. There she was no longer cold, and Paul seemed happy once more. After a time Paul fell asleep, and Polly carried him back into the room and put him to bed.

Polly, however, was still uncomfortable. Even with the heat turned up, she couldn't seem to get warm, and she felt a strangeness about the room. Nevertheless, having driven to Monterey from San Francisco after their flight from Chicago, she and her husband were exhausted, and they soon followed Paul to bed.

A short time later, Paul awoke and began crying and indicating that he wanted to get out of the room. Nothing Polly could do would quiet him. Still concerned about disturbing other guests, and bothered by the feeling that they weren't alone in the room, Polly hurriedly dressed and woke up her husband (who was not as affected by the feelings as she and Paul were). After telling him that she was taking Paul down to the lobby, she picked up her son and left the room. Once they were in the hall, Paul calmed down and fell asleep with his head resting on her shoulder.

As Polly made her way down a flight of stairs that led to the lobby and the quarterdeck (originally the hotel's main entrance and registration area), she felt a presence behind her. As the hair on the back of her neck started to rise, Paul also sensed something and woke up. Looking behind them, he pointed and began to "talk" to some unknown presence, just as he had done in room 211.

Afraid to look behind her, Polly quickened her pace and hurried to the bottom of the stairs. When she reached the quarterdeck, she told the two men who were on duty there about her experiences. It was from them that she learned, for the first time, about accounts of other ghostly happenings in the building, including tales of the Hotel Del Monte's most famous spirit, the Man in Gray. Interestingly, Polly reported that one of the two men didn't believe in the facility's ghosts, while the other most certainly did, even refusing to go into certain parts of the structure.

After a time Paul again fell asleep in his mother's arms, and the two of them were escorted back to their room by the fellow who believed the building was haunted. As Polly started to carry Paul into the room, he awoke again and began to cry. Leaving the door open, Polly proceeded to walk back and forth from the hall to the room, gently rocking her son. Finally, thinking about what her escort from the quarterdeck had told her, she started to talk to the presence. "Please leave the baby alone," she said. "He needs his sleep." By this time it was around 4 a.m. Shortly after making her request, she was relieved to see her son calm down and drift off to sleep.

Gratefully, Polly went back to bed. About an hour later, however, she was again awakened by Paul, who was making a series of strange sounds. Upon glancing at him she was shocked to see that even though he was in a sleep stupor, one of his arms was being lifted up in the air, "as if someone were pulling it to wake him up." Sitting up in bed, Polly forcefully spoke to the presence, telling it to please leave her son alone and let him sleep. Soon things quieted down, and what little was left of the night passed peacefully.

As the interview continued and Polly tried to express her feelings about what had taken place, she said that she felt "a sense of sadness." It was as if the presence didn't want to hurt Paul, but simply wanted to play with him.

She went on to say that even though Paul cried and was uncomfortable in the room, he wasn't afraid of the presence and his cries weren't cries of fear. In fact, at times he pointed to where the presence apparently was, and tried to go to it.

At this point, in checking my tape of our conversation, I think one of Polly's observations is most insightful. When she was expressing her feelings about the unseen presence, and the coldness that she felt, she mentioned that she was the only one who felt the cold and that "maybe Paul was *seeing* what I was *feeling*."

Before bringing this account to a close, I want to add a few additional comments that Polly made. In reference to the coldness Polly felt in the room, she compared it to the coldness she was familiar with in her home city of Chicago. Also, at the time of the interview Polly and her family had stayed in room 211 for three nights, but it was only on the first night that the coldness, and the presence, caused a problem. Polly's husband, while convinced that something odd was going on that first night, didn't pick up the same "vibes" that Polly and Paul did.

In reminiscing about her experience, Polly stated that she felt more annoyed than threatened. As I indicated earlier, she also said that she feels a sadness when she thinks about the presence, so much so that when she tried to describe it she started to cry. Part of her sadness is prompted by the feeling that the presence was lonely, and only wanted someone to play with.

A couple of other details Polly mentioned included the hall exit light on the second floor starting to blink when Paul approached it, and the television set in their room switching off by itself. Both of these incidents occurred on the first night.

Polly even came up with a Postgraduate School ghost story I wasn't aware of, which she heard from one of the school's workers while she was walking Paul in the hall. It seems that this fellow was busily folding and stacking towels and blankets in a second-floor storage room when he heard the door slam shut. Upon going to investigate, he discovered that no one was there. However, when he returned to where he had been working, the towels and blankets that he had just stacked were all strewn about!

Author's Note: A week after recording the preceding account, I was driving in Monterey when I spotted an old friend, a motorcycle policeman who had once held a very responsible position at the Naval Postgraduate School complex. It was he who turned me on to one of the most amazing ghost stories I have ever been involved with, recounted in "The Man in Gray pleaded for her help . . ." in *Ghost Notes.* Flagging him down, I proceeded to tell him about Polly's experiences at the old hotel.

"Yeah," he replied, "and I bet she was staying in room 212!" In reality, of course, Polly's room (211) was next door. When I asked why he had guessed room 212, he indicated that other people had also experienced strange things there, including the feeling of cold spots! He went on to say that in the early years of the Postgraduate School one of the top-ranking officers at the institution had died in (or near) the room.

After a pause, my friend reminded me that the lady who was involved in the "Man in Gray" incident some ten years earlier had had another strange experience at the facility in May of the same year (as related in "His ghostly presence was with them . . ." in *Ghost Notes*). "So what has that got to do with rooms 211 and 212?" I asked. He laughed and said, "Go home and listen to your tape of what happened that night."

Following his suggestion, I listened to the tape and was surprised to hear that on this second occasion, the lady—who was again in touch with the Man in Gray—had referred to him as Jason, and had indicated that he was staying in room 212! With my curiosity aroused, I checked with a member of the quarterdeck crew. Consulting his chart, he informed me that not only were rooms 211 and 212 next to each other, but there was a door ("which we never use") connecting the rooms!

The curse of James Dean's Spyder . . .

April 8, 1994 While on our way to San Luis Obispo (after I had given a series of talks in California's Central Valley city of Visalia), my wife and I stopped by the Jack Ranch Cafe in Cholame, on Highway 46 approximately twenty-four miles east of Paso Robles. It was within a few hundred yards of this roadside stop that movie actor James Dean was killed in an automobile accident on September 30, 1955. Today there is a memorial to the film star outside the cafe, and each year hundreds of the actor's fans flock to the site in the last week of September to commemorate his death.

Being at the cafe reminded me of the day back in 1981 when I got a call from the writer Richard Winer (author of *The Devil's Triangle,* and, with Nancy Osborn, *Haunted Houses*). Soon Richard and I were drinking coffee and discussing such things as wrecked ships, fast cars, and strange happenings. Qualifying on two accounts was the James Dean accident—which Richard wrote about in *Haunted Houses*—and the "life" his silver-gray 1955 Porsche Spyder took on after the actor's death. If you've ever read Stephen King's *Christine* (or seen the movie), James Dean's Spyder might be the real-life counterpart to the demented car featured in that work.

The Dean car evidently showed signs of a personality even before the tragic accident, judging by the accounts of certain people who worked on the vehicle or happened to be around it. Reportedly, they were awed by its power and the feelings of doom it generated. Today we can only wonder if these feelings were, in fact, predictors of things to come.

The accident that claimed Dean's life took place as he was speeding toward the Monterey County community of Salinas, where he was to race the next day. (Besides being a famous young actor, Dean was also a promising amateur sports-car driver.) Unfortunately, destiny had other plans,

70

as instead of cruising into Salinas, Dean and his Spyder tangled with a behemoth American sedan on a stretch of Highway 46, a two-lane road then known as Route 466. The wreckage of both the Porsche and the sedan were hauled to the grounds of the Jack Ranch Cafe, where they rested for a time in a building directly west of the restaurant.

It wasn't until the Spyder's remains were purchased for parts by a well-known southern California garage owner and car designer that its life of gloom and doom made people take notice. Was the James Dean car cursed? Let me simply list some of the incidents associated with the vehicle so you can decide for yourself.

1. While the wrecked Porsche was being unloaded from the truck it was transported on, the car slipped and broke a mechanic's leg (or legs, depending on the source).

2. The Spyder's engine was sold to a doctor who raced sports cars. The doctor was killed the first time he raced the vehicle with the Dean engine in it.

3. Part of the Porsche's drive train was sold to a second doctor who also raced sports cars. The first time he competed in the car after the Spyder parts were installed, it locked up and flipped for no apparent reason. The doctor was badly injured in the accident.

4. The rear tires that were on the Porsche at the time of Dean's wreck were undamaged. However, after being sold to a sports car enthusiast, within a week both tires blew out—at the exact same time. According to at least one source, the driver sustained multiple injuries in the accident that followed.

And that's not all. When the California Highway Patrol (and various other law-enforcement agencies across the country) started using Dean's wrecked car as part of a traveling safety display, a series of strange and in some cases tragic events continued to plague the vehicle or the people who were involved with it. Here are some examples.

1. When the car was stored in a California Highway Patrol garage (for display the next day), the garage caught fire. All of the automobiles in the building were destroyed—except for the Spyder, which suffered only minor paint damage.

2. While on display in Sacramento the car fell from its stand, breaking a teenager's hip.

3. While the car was being transported by truck to Salinas (the same destination Dean was heading for at the time of his accident), the truck driver lost control of his vehicle. In the wreck that followed, he was thrown from his rig. Breaking loose from its mounts during the accident, the Spyder crashed into the truck driver and killed him.

4. While on display in New Orleans, the car suddenly broke into eleven pieces. Upon inspection no reason could be found for the breaks.

5. After being exhibited by the Florida Highway Patrol, the Porsche was prepared for shipping and sent back to its California owner. Unfortunately, the car vanished in route. As to what became of the vehicle . . . your guess is as good as mine.

Musing over all this as I remembered my conversation with Richard Winer (whose accounts and book I have to thank for much of the preceding information), I decided to ask around and see if there were any ghost stories connected with the Jack Ranch Cafe. Upon tracking down a woman who had worked at the restaurant longer than anyone else, I asked whether anything strange or hard to explain had ever taken place there. After thinking for a moment, she nodded and said that after the Dean accident people would see the reflection of an automobile's headlights in the windows of the cafe, but when they turned to look in the direction the vehicle was coming, there was never a car there!

Now, I'm not suggesting that these episodes connect with the brilliant actor's death. But the fact remains that in the examples she gave me, the car was always traveling in the same direction as the Dean car, at about the same time as the accident (around dusk). And of course, it was the building next to the restaurant that once housed the wrecked Spyder . . .

With the aid of a Ouija board . . .

April 8, 1994 After our stop at the Jack Ranch Cafe, my wife and I continued on to San Luis Obispo, where we spent the night. After checking into our motel, I decided to look into a story I had heard about a ghost that was said to frequent a local restaurant. So, included in our evening's schedule was a stop at the popular eatery known as This Old House.

Located outside of town on the Los Osos end of Foothill Boulevard, the restaurant (at least the original part of it) occupies an old farmhouse that dates back to about 1917. It wasn't until 1950 that the structure became an eating establishment. Since that time many stories have been told about the building, including several ghostly tales.

With the aid of a Ouija board, it was learned that one "presence" in residence at This Old House was a man by the name of John Vittey. Apparently Vittey was born in Georgia, but moved to California from the town of Autry, Utah.

Various theories have been offered to explain why John's ghost lingers about the premises. One worker indicated that Mr. Vittey had been employed by the building's owner and had died in a fire that had taken place there. If this account is true, perhaps it was near the restaurant's central section that John met his end, as according to workers, as well as some customers, it is in that area that his presence is most often felt.

Other than a presence, other unexplained happenings at the establishment have included chairs moving on their own, lights flashing for no reason, moans and squeaks that come in spurts, a jukebox that turns on and off by itself (and that always plays the same song), sightings of people and the sound of voices when no one is there, pots and pans that rattle in an empty kitchen, mysterious cool winds that blow through certain parts of the building, toilet-paper rolls that unroll by themselves, an oven that heated up to 600 degrees after the gas was turned off, and fireplace pokers that swing back and forth even after people reach out and stop them.

Oh, yes, according to one worker I chatted with, a Ouija board also indicated that the ghost of a young girl frequents the place. Perhaps it is her playful presence that moves the fireplace pokers, plays the jukebox, and unrolls the toilet paper. Whatever the explanation may be, the good news is that all of the ghosts who inhabit or visit the establishment are said to be friendly and to never cause anybody any harm.

Both parties confirmed the girl's presence . . .

July 21, 1994 Located approximately fifteen miles south of San Luis Obispo, the town of Arroyo Grande is not one of Highway 101's major tourist attractions. But ever since I learned about a little girl's ghost that haunts one of the community's prized Victorians, I have wanted to visit the site. So, while driving south from the Monterey Peninsula

74

I stopped by the town and found my way to the aged edifice.

Known as the Rose Victorian Inn, the structure is something of a landmark and has operated for several years as a restaurant and bed and breakfast inn. Viewed from the street (Valley Road), the establishment is most impressive, as it dwarfs all of the other buildings in the area.

Other than its park-like grounds, perhaps the most imposing part of the 100-plus-year-old house is its four-story tower. It is here that the little girl's ghost has most often been seen.

According to the most credible account, the young lady was about nine when she died at the site as the result of a flu epidemic that swept through the area in 1918. At the time of her death the girl, like many children who lived in elaborate houses of that time, had a favorite room where she kept her things. It was in this room—in the tower—that she spent much of her time, and it is here that her ghost is said to linger.

Early in 1983 a husband and wife ghost-hunting team visited the building and stayed overnight. Later that same year another ghost hunter (who is well known in the field and writes books about the subject) also visited the house. Working independently, both parties confirmed the girl's presence. Reportedly, without comparing notes or discussing their findings with each other, the ghost hunters agreed on such things as the youngster's age, the color of her hair, the kind of dress she wore, and the time period in which she died.

Several of the inn's guests have also commented on the presence of the ghost. Some are shocked, as they have never experienced such things, while others merely nod and accept the fact that they are sharing their quarters with a delightful young lady of long ago.

Incidentally, a descendant of the family who occupied the dwelling at the time of the girl's death indicated that such an event *did* take place . . . and that the child's name was believed to be Elaine. If this is right, the ghost hunters were not far off, as they offered such names as Ellen, Alicia, Alaine, and Alice.

As for the owners of the house, even though they have never seen the ghost, they are certainly aware of it! They have also observed evidence of its presence in the Tower Room, where, they say, the pillows have been rearranged by unseen hands, and, on occasion, the bed looks like it has been sat on when no one has been in the room. The owners have made no effort to rid the structure of the ghost, as they think it is happy there (a supposition at least partially confirmed by one of the ghost hunters), and it has not created any *major* disturbances among the guests.

In closing I might add that a neighbor claims there may be more than one ghost in the building. He reports that at night, when the house is empty, he can sometimes see a man peering at him from behind a coat rack in a second-story room. As we talked he pointed out the rack, but it was mid-afternoon when we chatted, and neither he nor I could make out any sign of a ghost on that bright, sunny day.

A gown of white . . .

October 14, 1994 In *Ghost Notes,* I related how some of the sightings at the U.S. Naval Postgraduate School in Monterey (the old Hotel Del Monte) concern a lady dressed in a gown of white. Today I ran across some new information that may bear on these accounts.

While I was checking out the facility's museum in preparation for a community-college class I was scheduled to teach there, I saw a copy of *The Monterey New Era* newspaper, dated April 18, 1906. The paper reported that a Mr. and Mrs. Rouzer were on their bridal tour when they were killed at the Del Monte by a falling chimney (as well as debris from the roof) during the famous San Francisco earthquake. Mr. Rouzer was described as the manager of the Copper Queen Hotel in Bisbee (presumably the copper-mining town in Arizona). The couple were staying in room 97, on the third floor of the main building, just above the office. According to the newspaper, at least fifteen of the hotel's twenty-five chimneys "came crashing to the ground" during the quake.

While this information confirms the long-standing story of an out-of-state couple who lost their lives at the hotel during the 1906 earthquake, it was a more recent caption above the article that caught my attention. The caption indicated that the Rouzers were a "young couple" who were staying in the honeymoon suite at the time of the tragedy. However, of most interest to me was the caption's last sentence, which read, "Since that time, several guests have reported seeing a young woman in an unusual wedding dress beckon to them."

With this information in mind, I can't help but wonder whether the apparition of the "young woman" is connected with the other Hotel Del Monte sightings of a lady attired in a gown of white that I have already recorded . . .

Author's Note: The sightings referred to above are recounted in several sections of Ghost Notes: "The Man in Gray pleaded for her help . . . ," "The elevator was empty . . . ," and "The man was wielding an axe . . . ."

Ghostly happenings aboard the Queen Mary . . .

November 4, 1994 While staying at the Hyatt Regency in Long Beach, where I was presenting a session at the annual conference of the California Reading Association, I enjoyed a room overlooking the Long Beach harbor and the magnificent ocean liner *Queen Mary*. Having heard of several ghostly happenings aboard the vessel, and knowing that she was celebrating her Diamond Jubilee (having been built in 1934), I decided it was only appropriate that I visit the ship. So, within the hour I was aboard the luxurious liner.

One psychic has said that the *Queen Mary* is "one of the most haunted places in the country." Certainly there is no shortage of ghostly tales associated with the venerable vessel. Among the many stories are those that tell of a crew member's ghost that has been observed in the ship's Shaft Alley (where he was crushed to death) . . . of wet footprints (and ghosts clad in bathing suits) that have been spotted near the First Class Pool when it is empty of water . . . of the ghost of Senior 2nd Officer W. E. Stark, who is said to haunt his old quarters . . . of a lovely lady ghost who is always seen wearing a white evening gown when she dances, alone, in the First Class Main Lounge . . . and, certainly not least, of the ghostly spirit of the vessel's first captain (Sir Edgar Britten), who is rumored to watch over and protect his beloved ship.

Upon touring the vessel, I was greatly impressed by its size and its Old World elegance. Our tour guide, however, pooh-poohed many of the ghost stories, indicating that several of the strange happenings—particularly "unexplained" noises such as the banging and clattering of pipes—were nothing more than the normal sounds of a ship. Interestingly, though, one of the people taking the tour, a pilot for an international airline, disagreed with the guide. Suggesting that there was more to the stories than the guide was willing to admit, the pilot proceeded to tell about the flight attendants who used to stay at the Hotel Queen Mary when his company flew out of the Long Beach airport. (Today the grand old vessel serves as a first-class hotel boasting many fine restaurants and more than 350 rooms.) Because so many peculiar things happened to them—and to the ship itself—when they were staying there, the flight attendants refused to be booked back aboard the vessel!

Taken together with the many better-known stories about the *Queen Mary*, the pilot's remarks can only make one wonder whether our guide was telling all that he knew about the liner's colorful collection of ghosts.

The Big Yellow House of Santa Barbara County . . .

April 28, 1995 As one of four authors who participated this week in Santa Barbara County's 26th Annual Author-Go-Round, I was privileged to meet with over one hundred different students each day from all over the county. The students were in the fourth through the eighth grades, and were chosen by their teachers to participate in the event on the basis of their ability, enthusiasm, and writing talent. Even though most of our time was taken up with discussions about writing, we also exchanged a number of ghost stories.

Judging from the students' accounts, one of the best-known "ghostly houses" along the Santa Barbara coast seems to be a huge, old yellow building located slightly south of the city of Santa Barbara. Visible from Highway 101, today the dwelling is a popular restaurant known as the Big Yellow House.

After hearing about the structure from a number of students (and some adults), I decided to pay it a visit. While I was there I learned that the original house dates back to the 1880s. It was constructed by Henry L. Williams, a spiritualist from the Atlantic side of the United States who also acquired the nearby town of Ortega. Renaming the region Summerland, Williams dreamed of turning it into a center for "spiritualistic living."

Sadly, Williams died in 1899, and his dream of a spiritualistic community bordering the Pacific died with him. However, various individuals who are familiar with the history of the house wonder whether the ghostly happenings that are attributed to it can be traced to the facility's spiritualistic beginnings.

Interestingly, not far from his house Williams built a second structure that served as a gathering place and recreation center for the people of Summerland. Besides hosting parties and dances that attracted people from throughout the county, the building was also the site of several séances. Because of this, and because a number of mediums and psychics held their meetings there, the facility became known to local non-spiritualists as "Spook Hall."

Today Spook Hall is little more than a memory, but the original Williams residence (The Big Yellow House) is said to more than make up for it, as mediums, séances, and "spooky" happenings are all a part of its history. One medium who stayed there for lengthy periods of time, and who became a favorite of the Williams children, was a gifted woman of French descent. Among her many talents was one that especially endeared her to the children—the ability to send her "spiritual guide" to the pasture whenever they desired to go horseback riding. In this way, no matter how far out to pasture the animals were, when the children got to the corral the horses would come to them and willingly let themselves be prepared for riding.

While séances were relatively common at the Williams house in the early days, as time went by—and the house experienced changes in both design and use—its history of odd occurrences took on a decidedly different air. Mediums and séances were observed less and less, and more in the way of ghostly happenings were reported.

Some of the building's best-known early ghost stories were told about the basement. In fact, many years ago rumors stated that the ghost of a mentally retarded child haunted the cellar. Accounts even indicated that bars had been put on the basement windows when the child was alive to keep him from getting out. However, research (not to mention common sense) suggests that the bars were put on the cellar windows to keep people out, not in.

Other tales relating to the basement are of more recent vintage. Among these are the relatively common occurrences of lights flickering and going out, loud noises being heard (including the crash of a bottle breaking, though neither broken glass nor bottle could be found), and a distinct feeling of presence that, at times, seemed to fill the cellar. The presence has been felt by several people, with one worker reporting that when the feeling was the strongest he "could follow the spirit around the room."

The basement certainly doesn't have a monopoly on ghosts, as feelings of presence, as well as an assortment of odd happenings, have also been experienced in various upstairs rooms. One example was reported by workers in the parking lot who observed lights turning on and off in the Orange Room when the house was empty. A second example takes us to the Red Room, where the door, and its knob, rattled and shook as if someone was trying to get into the room. Of course, no one was there.

According to a Santa Barbara medium who visited the site, the Red Room was also the scene of a gathering of black people. When observed the group was around a fire listening to a large black man. The man appeared to be leading some kind of a religious meeting or ritual. Unfortunately, the medium was unable to ascertain either the significance of the gathering or who the people were.

Among several other rumors that have circulated about the house is one that told of windows that opened and closed by themselves. Another mentioned dishes in the upstairs Library Room that were found broken when no one had been in the room to break them. One of the waitresses got into the act by describing how her skirt had been pulled by an unseen thing.

My favorite tale concerns the restaurant manager who walked into one of the dining rooms early one morning and found all the tables stacked on top of each other and reaching to the ceiling! If this wasn't enough to give him pause, upon investigating he discovered that all of the tables were set—complete with tablecloths, napkins, and silverware!

One of the past owners appeared before her . . .

June 5, 1995 While in California's Gold Country, my wife and I stayed at one of Sutter Creek's best-known bed and breakfast inns, an establishment that was built in the 1860s. After renewing my acquaintance with the owner, a delightful lady in her seventies, I was treated to the tale of a strange and beautiful ghostly happening.

One afternoon, the owner told me, she was in one of the main downstairs rooms when one of the past owners—a well-known gentleman who lived in the house during the late 1800s—appeared before her and told her how pleased he was with the way the facility was being cared for. In continuing, he assured her that he would watch over and protect the house. With that, his image vanished as quickly as it had appeared.

The owner would rather not publicize the fact that the establishment has (or had) a ghost, as, in her words, "Some people associate ghosts with evil." For this reason I promised that I wouldn't mention the name of the inn. However, I will say that if you happen upon it in your travels, you are in for a real treat. My wife summed up the feeling of warmth and security we experienced when she opened the door to our room after a day of Gold Country wanderings and said she felt like she was "coming home."

He saw the ghostly figure of a woman . . .

July 7, 1995 Several days ago, at a wedding reception in the Santa Cruz County community of Aptos, I got to talking with a Monterey Peninsula actor who had played the role of Robert Louis Stevenson in several of Monterey's centennial observances of Stevenson's death. During the conversation, the actor mentioned a respected local merchant who, he said, was one of several people who had told him of ghostly encounters at the Robert Louis Stevenson House.

Today I ran into the merchant at a Monterey-area post office. He told me that his ghostly experience had occurred several years ago, when he was touring the Stevenson House with some friends. Fascinated by the aged adobe and the antique furnishings in the upstairs rooms, he was surprised—perhaps shocked is a better word—when he peered into the children's nursery and saw the ghostly figure of a woman! Awed by the sight, as he had never seen a ghost before, he sought out his friends, who were admiring items in other rooms, and told them about the woman. Unfortunately, by the time they got to the nursery, the image had disappeared.

That evening, when he and his friends were having dinner with his family, the subject of the ghost came up. The merchant was surprised to learn that, several years before, his mother had also seen the ghostly figure of a woman at the Stevenson House.

The merchant went on to say that he had learned that the ghost's last name was Sanchez (or something similar), and that long before she had been killed at the site (he thinks she was stabbed).

This brief account piqued my interest in part because of the possible link between the merchant's experience and the story I related in *Ghost Notes* of a woman who was killed on or near the back steps of the Stevenson House. (See "He drew his blade . . ." and "A woman was

83

killed on or near the back steps . . . .") That death was due to a knife wound, and is rumored to have taken place around the turn of the century. Could the woman I described in *Ghost Notes* have been named Sanchez? Could there be a connection between the *Ghost Notes* stories and the merchant's sighting? Sadly, we will probably never know.

He saw something that shouldn't have been there . . .

July 7, 1995 After the merchant in the preceding note told me about his Stevenson House experience, he went on to describe a "really weird" happening he had been involved in. Several years ago, he explained, he became good friends with the father of an employee who worked at a second store he owned in Santa Cruz. Sadly, the father became ill and was placed in a Santa Cruz hospital. The merchant visited him as often as he could, and encouraged the man's son to do the same. One day, after the father had taken a turn for the worse, the merchant was working in his Peninsula store when he was overcome by an odd feeling about his friend. Thinking the end might be near, he called the man's son and told him to hurry to the hospital. The son replied that he couldn't go then because the store was full of people. "Forget the people!" responded the merchant. Promising to cover for his employee, he admonished him to "go to the hospital— now!"

Obeying his boss, the son worked out a way to leave the store and made a beeline for the hospital. In the meantime the merchant left his Peninsula store and headed for Santa Cruz to cover for the son. When he was about halfway there, he suddenly sensed he was no longer alone in his car. Glancing over his shoulder, he saw something that shouldn't have been there. Frantically spinning around for a second look, he saw his friend on the back seat!

Even more remarkably, the apparition began to speak. He didn't know what was happening to him, the man said, but he did know that he didn't hurt any more. He went on to say that he was going to be able to "stay around" (perhaps in spirit form) until his son's wife had her baby. Finally, before disappearing, the man added that the baby was going to be a healthy little girl.

A short time after the merchant arrived at his Santa Cruz store, the son came by and told him that his dad had died. In thanking his boss for calling him, the son added that it was only because of the call that he had been there when the end came. Somehow the merchant was not surprised to learn that his friend had died at approximately the time he had seen him in the back of his car.

Before parting, the merchant asked the son whether his wife was pregnant. Looking at him strangely, the son shook his head and joked, "Why? Are you trying to tell me something?" With a laugh the merchant muttered a reply and dropped the subject.

A couple of weeks later, the son called to tell his boss that he and his wife had just learned that they were expecting a baby! When the baby was born, it turned out to be a healthy little girl—just as the merchant's friend had predicted.

In closing I would like to add that it seems fitting that the baby was named after her grandfather, the man whose ghost had looked into the future and foreseen her birth!

Perhaps General Vallejo's ghost is still with us . . .

July 21, 1995 While on a trip to northern California's Sonoma Valley, my wife and I stopped off in the town of Sonoma, home of California's northernmost mission and the site of the Bear Flag Revolt in 1846. While we were there we visited several of the historic buildings, including the elegant old home of the respected Mexican general Mariano Guadalupe Vallejo. Today the structure is state-owned and open to the public.

As a follow-up to a conversation I had had on a previous visit to the Vallejo home, I asked a couple of workers at the site about a ghostly presence that supposedly haunts the building. Responding enthusiastically, they talked about how General Vallejo's spirit is said to watch over the house and how it has been seen or felt by a number of people who have visited the site. In addition, they shared some tales of past employees who had experienced strange happenings of their own.

Several such incidents were experienced by a carpenter who did some restoration work on the building. Among the things that he reported was the movement of tools from the areas in which he was working. Not only did certain tools move just as he reached for them (making it difficult for him to complete his assigned tasks), but on more than one occasion his hammer mysteriously fell from the roof, requiring him to vacate his precarious perch and reclaim his hammer from the gardens two stories below.

Another incident involved one of the estate's gardeners. On numerous occasions when he was alone on the grounds, he felt a presence when he was near the main house. Each time he also heard a voice bidding him good morning. Interestingly, the greeting was always in Spanish, and sounded like it had been spoken by a man of culture.

Perhaps the most interesting account that was shared with me concerned one of the very workers I was talking to. Upon checking the main house late one afternoon prior to locking it for the night—and after having been told by some visitors that there was a definite presence in the structure—she stood in the main entryway and said out loud, "General Vallejo, if you are here, please move something or show me in some way that you are about." At that exact moment one of the doors near her began to swing shut! What makes this more than mere coincidence is the fact that she had just checked the building, and no doors or windows were open to create a draft.

So, who knows . . . perhaps General Vallejo's ghost is still with us. Maybe he's still trying to figure out what the Bear Flaggers were about when they captured him on that June day in 1846 and hustled him off to Sutter's Fort in what we now know as Sacramento. After all, he was sympathetic to the Americans and fully expected the Stars and Stripes to someday fly over his northern California land.

Unfortunately, his wife was dead . . .

October 12, 1995 While signing books after giving a talk at Monterey's Naval Postgraduate School, I met a couple of ladies who had an interesting account to share about a house in nearby Carmel Valley.

It seems that the house had been purchased by one of the professors at the Postgraduate School. According to the ladies' account, the house had been for sale for quite some time, but no one had bought it because of several strange tales that were connected with it. However, the stories didn't detract from the dwelling for the professor and her family, and they made an offer on it. The man who owned the building said he needed to discuss the offer with his wife and that he would get back to them.

A few days later the owner called and said that he and his wife agreed that the professor's family were "right" for the house. In fact, he said, they were so pleased that they had decided to take $100,000 off the price!

Ecstatic over this news, the professor asked the man to put his wife on the phone so she could thank her. He replied that, unfortunately, that wouldn't be possible, because she was dead! After a moment the owner went on to say that there was also one stipulation that the professor and her family would have to agree to. Still awestruck by the man's comment about his wife, the professor mumbled something about how sorry she was to learn of her death, and then somewhat hesitatingly asked what the stipulation was.

The owner's response was so bizarre that once again the professor was struck speechless. Every year for the next five years, the owner said, the house had to be vacated for the first two weeks of August. It was during this time, he explained, that he communicated with his wife. Furthermore, the furnishings would have to remain just as they were when the family was there. To make the deal more appealing, the owner added that he would pay for the family to stay at one of Carmel Valley's most elegant inns during the time they were out of the house.

Even though the professor and her family were dumbfounded by the request—and its obvious implications about the house—they were so impressed with the dwelling (not to mention the fantastic price they were getting it for), that they decided to go ahead with the deal.

As the two ladies were sharing this remarkable account with me, a third lady walked up to the table behind them and nodded in agreement to everything they said. As it turned out, it was she who had purchased the house! When the two ladies finished their story, she smiled and handed me her card. "It's all true," she assured me. "If you have any questions, please give me a call."

As I record this account, the professor and her family are just getting settled in the house. So far everything is fine. Of course, August has already come and gone for this year . . .

She had drowned long ago . . .

October 28, 1995 Today I was treated to a story while dropping off some books at the Asilomar Conference Grounds. Asilomar is a state-owned, park-like facility that borders the Pacific Ocean between Pebble Beach and Pacific Grove. It is internationally known, and its conferences attract participants from throughout the world. Apparently this lovely setting also attracts ghosts, as I had already recorded an account about the ghost of an elderly Oriental man who had occasionally been seen in the "Chinese house" just outside the conference grounds (see "He always appears in a yellow robe . . ." in *Ghost Notes*). Today I learned of other spectral visitors from one of the administrative staff.

According to this lady, among the buildings that supposedly have ghosts in them are the chapel and the main hall. Both of these structures were built in the 1920s, and both were designed by the famed architect Julia Morgan, who is perhaps best known for her work in designing Hearst Castle.

The story that affected her the most, the administrator told me, involved a little girl who had been seen on the meadow in front of the Administration Building (also of Julia Morgan design), dressed in clothes of 1920s vintage. Asked why she was there, she replied that she keeps coming back to the meadow because that's where she "had the most fun." Upon further questioning she revealed that she had drowned long ago at Asilomar Beach (then known as Moss Beach), only a short distance from the meadow.

A haunted school in Santa Clara County . . .

January 13, 1996 After giving a talk at the annual conference of the Santa Clara County Reading Council, I was busily signing books when a principal from the Sunnyvale School District stopped by my table and began telling me about a ghost that frequented her school. The principal indicated that most of the people at the school who were familiar with the happenings were of the opinion that the apparition was the ghost of either the well-known architect who had designed the building or the man who had previously owned the property (the latter had once been a large land owner in Santa Clara County).

Among the happenings the principal described were odd and unexplainable sounds that emanated from the attic or the auditorium's projector room. It was also in the auditorium that doors banged of their own accord. The unexplainable sounds and the banging of the doors have been witnessed by people from both inside and outside of the building. On one occasion, after a union meeting was held at the site, the union president was struck by a door as he was leaving the facility. Since no one was near the door at the time, perhaps some wise soul will surmise that it was a *non-union* ghost who was responsible for the incident!

Upon taking her leave, the principal invited me to the school to talk to the teachers and other individuals who have experienced the ghost, especially the librarian (within whose room a mysterious white cloud has been seen and photographed). So, I will add this school to my ever-lengthening list of haunted sites that warrant a visit.

Unholy happenings at Monterey's Royal Presidio Chapel . . .

March 30, 1996 Two historic buildings that I've written about in several other publications are the Royal Presidio Chapel on Church Street in Monterey (which is more than two hundred years old) and its aged rectory (which now houses offices, storage facilities, and a small gift shop). As these buildings are well known to ghost enthusiasts, I was not surprised to learn from a respected woman who works in them that unholy happenings continue to take place within the two structures.

One of the most recent incidents experienced in the chapel was the sighting of a "candle-like light" that moved about the choir loft. The sighting was made by two teenaged boys who, with the blessing of the priest, had entered the chapel to practice their trumpet playing in preparation for an upcoming event. It was while they were intent on their music that they spotted the light. Knowing they were supposedly the only ones in the church, they promptly dropped their trumpets and left the building on the run.

The chapel's old rectory next door is even better known as far as ghostly occurrences are concerned. My informant added to my collection of tales with an account that was told to her by a couple who had been doing some cleaning on the rectory's ground floor. Knowing they were alone in the building, and hearing repeated footsteps on the main staircase, the woman poked her head out of the room she was in and called to her husband, asking why he kept going up and down the stairs. Responding from a second room some distance from the staircase, the husband insisted that he hadn't been near the stairs, and that he had thought the footsteps were hers. Interestingly, phantom footsteps on the old rectory's main staircase have reportedly been heard for more than fifty years . . .

The Blue Lady of Moss Beach . . .

April 27, 1996 Several days ago, knowing that I would be passing through the community of Moss Beach (near Half Moon Bay, south of San Francisco) on my way from a wedding reception, I phoned the popular Moss Beach Distillery restaurant to see whether there was any truth to the ghost stories I had heard about the place. During a delightful chat with the hostess, she confirmed that one or more ghosts are thought to frequent the establishment. The spirit that she referred to as the building's best-known ghost is the "Blue Lady," whose presence has been seen or felt by countless people over a period of many years.

The hostess suggested that I stop by the restaurant and talk to some of the workers who had experienced ghostly happenings. This comment prompted me to ask whether she herself had experienced anything out of the ordinary while working at the facility. Between answering a second phone and escorting customers to tables, she managed to tell me about one of several unexplained incidents that happened to her.

The event she described took place in the downstairs women's restroom. Being the only one downstairs at the time (as the restaurant had closed for the night), the hostess entered one of the restroom stalls. The stalls, she explained, had pairs of swinging doors on them whose latches were sometimes difficult to fasten. With considerable effort she secured the latch and sat down. Suddenly, for no apparent reason, the latch burst from its door, and the doors violently swung toward her, as if someone had given them a mighty push! Shocked and somewhat shaken, she immediately vacated the stall, glanced around the restroom, and ran upstairs. Convinced that she had been the only person in the restroom at the time, the hostess had little choice but to chalk the experience up to the building's Blue Lady or one of her ghostly friends.

With this as my introduction to the Moss Beach Distillery, I decided to take the hostess's advice and visit the establishment on my way home from the wedding reception. Today I paid my promised visit to the Distillery. I soon learned that it boasts quite a colorful history, including accounts of bootlegging and boat chasing in its distant past. The structure, which dates back to pre-

Depression days, is perched on a bluff overlooking the Pacific, a location as dramatic as it is picturesque. With this as its setting, I must admit that the building lends itself to spooky happenings, as ghostly blankets of drifting fog often engulf the bluff and everything on it. Some people might be prone to say that any uncomfortable feelings and eerie sounds are nothing more than the product of fog and ocean winds, but, after being shown about the establishment and meeting with several of its workers, I can't help but think that there are more to the stories than fog-induced visions and wind-created sounds.

Included in the workers' accounts are a number of incidents in which objects were reported to have moved on their own. One such tale told of three receipt books that flew from a rack above the bar to a spot on the bar approximately three feet away. Only two people (both workers) were in the bar at the time, and both witnessed the event. A second account was relayed by a waitress who was on the back deck when one of the chairs moved (as if it was being dragged) a distance of about five feet. No wind was blowing when the incident took place, and none of the other identically matched chairs moved. A third story concerned a bartender who claimed to have seen several objects teeter and fall when no one was near them to give them a push.

Among the other items shared with me during my visit was a brief account by a waitress who told of being "flicked" on the neck when she was alone in one of the upstairs rooms. A similar incident was reported by a second waitress, who felt "a tap on the back" in an empty room. This account prompted three other waitresses to share their own stories of similar experiences they had had in various rooms throughout the building. More traditional feelings of presence and peculiar sounds were also reported by a number of workers, coupled with several reports of odd happenings associated with the telephones.

This grouping of events was enough to whet my appetite and cause me to do some homework. Here are some of the things I learned about the Moss Beach Distillery and its best-known ghost, the mysterious Blue Lady.

According to legend (partially confirmed in aged newspaper reports), the original Blue Lady frequented the area sometime around 1920. Sadly, she was killed in a tragic automobile accident on the coast road. Already married, and the mother of one, the woman had fallen in love with a playboy-type fellow who was a regular—and possibly the piano player—at the popular Marine View Beach Hotel. (The hotel no longer exists, but at one time it shared the bluff with the Distillery building.)

Before meeting her end, the lovely young lady had several secret rendezvous with her lover at or near the oceanside hotel. Together they shared the sunsets, explored the bluffs, and walked on the nearby beaches. Reportedly the woman was always attired in blue, with some accounts indicating that she wore a veiled blue hat and matching gloves. It was this image that remained in people's minds long after her death. When her ghost was seen (perhaps looking for her lover) at the hotel/distillery sites, she continued to wear blue.

Interestingly, early-day gossip also indicates that the Blue Lady wasn't the only woman the playboy was seeing at the time. Heartbroken by the news of a second affair (which came to light after the Blue Lady's death), the second woman is said to have thrown herself into the sea. Today, her ghost is said to join the Blue Lady on the bluff. Some sources also say that the playboy himself has been known to make an appearance!

With three of the ghostly images that have been seen about the Distillery having been identified, how many others may also haunt the site remains an open question. Certainly any number of strange happenings have been reported at the establishment, including the following:

1. Doors have been bolted from the inside, requiring people to crawl through windows to open them.

2. A checkbook has been observed floating about a room.

3. Footsteps (apparently made by high-heeled shoes) and the sounds of tables and chairs being moved in upstairs rooms have been heard in the middle of the night.

4. Cases of wine in a locked wine room have been stacked from the inside against the room's only door, making it impossible to get in (or out) of the room without first moving the wine.

5. A shower has turned on in the middle of the night, when no one was near it.

I could go on with such things as names being whispered about, lights that mysteriously turn on and off, and the experiences of several children at the site (including sightings), but I think you get the picture. Suffice it to say that for ghost buffs the Moss Beach Distillery offers considerably more than fine food, beautiful views, and hardy spirits of the liquid kind.

The ghostly face peered from the window . . .

July 7, 1996 While I was autographing books at the Monterey Maritime Museum near Fisherman's Wharf, a young couple asked if I knew any ghost stories about the Salinas area. After I shared a couple of tales from *Ghost Notes,* they asked whether I knew anything about the ghost of a theater projectionist that haunted one of the old downtown theaters. When I shook my head no, they proceeded to tell me about a ghostly face that has been seen peering from the window of the theater's projection booth.

The couple had heard about the ghost from the building's owner, a friend of theirs who is one of several people who has seen the image. In telling about his sighting, he said that after the initial shock wore off he began checking around to see whether he could find out anything about it. Upon talking to the building's previous owner (who has also seen the image), he learned that many years before a projectionist had reportedly committed suicide in the booth with the aid of a rope and a trap door in the floor. Needless to say, the ghostly image that peers from the projection booth window is said to resemble that of the long-dead projectionist.

There may be more than fish in the Monterey Bay Aquarium . . .

July 18, 1996 As I have often said, I never know where the next ghost story will come from. Today it was the mail that brought me a tale, in the form of a letter from a lady in Oregon. In it she told me about a strange experience she had had on July 7 at the Monterey Bay Aquarium. As evidenced by my accounts in *Ghost Notes,* hers is far from the first experience that suggests there may be more than fish in the world-famous aquarium.

According to her letter, my correspondent's encounter took place in the morning, shortly after the aquarium opened. She and her husband and daughter were alone in the round room that serves as an entryway to the Outer Bay exhibit. As they stared at the huge tank that circled the room above them, they were awed by the thousands of anchovies that swam in one long, continuous stream around the tank. While they were engrossed in this remarkable exhibit, the lady felt someone place a hand on her shoulder and pull it down. She then heard a voice whisper in her ear and felt someone's breath on her hair. The voice was soft and spoke in a language she was unfamiliar with. Thinking that another tourist (perhaps from a foreign country) had entered the room while she was staring at the fish, she turned to see who was there. It was then that she realized that she and her family were still the only ones in the room. Startled and not a little bewildered, she asked her husband what had happened. When he responded by asking what she was talking about, she realized that she was the only one who had experienced the incident.

Feeling very unsettled, but not wanting to interrupt her family's visit, she told them to continue their tour and that she would meet them in the gift shop near the main entrance. (The gift shop, she explained, was full of people, and she felt safe there.) While she was browsing in the shop, she picked up a copy of *Ghost Notes* and turned to the index, where she saw a listing for the Monterey Bay Aquarium.

Upon reading the accounts, she realized that other people had experienced strange happenings at the aquarium that were different from hers. It was these stories that prompted her to write me about her encounter, hoping that her tale would "help shed additional light on the aquarium's hauntings."

The feelings were strongest in George Sterling's room . . .

September 6, 1996 Earlier I mentioned an aged house in Carmel that was one of the village's earliest inns and that was frequented by many important guests, particularly from the field of literature (see "A restless recluse . . . ," page 10). In May I visited the establishment, which is now a popular bed and breakfast inn, and was able to tour the facility at my own pace. Upon venturing upstairs I saw brass plaques mounted on some of the doors with names of prominent people inscribed on them. Among the names were those of the writers Sinclair Lewis, Mary Austin, Jack London, and George Sterling. According to the building's owner, the plaques commemorate individuals who had stayed in those rooms.

This brings us to today, and a visit to my favorite Pacific Grove coffeehouse. While waiting for a buddy to join me for a cup, I saw a woman whom I will call Elaine. She had previously worked at the Carmel inn and had briefly told me about a ghostly experience there. Fortunately my buddy was late, and Elaine had a chance to tell me more about her experience.

Early one morning, as was her custom, Elaine arrived at the inn before any of the guests were up and began straightening the living room and rekindling the fire. As the fire began to crackle and the room took on a friendly glow, she suddenly had the feeling that she wasn't alone. Turning about, she saw the ghostly image of an old woman sitting in the chair nearest the fire. Because the woman radiated a feeling of warmth and goodwill, Elaine wasn't afraid. After she had stared at the apparition for a short time, it suddenly dawned on her that the likeness matched that of the building's original owner—right down to the red dress that she wore. As the ghostly image continued to sit in the chair, apparently enjoying the surroundings and the warmth of the fire, Elaine could only smile to herself and feel good in knowing that the woman appeared to be pleased with her work and the way the house was being kept.

Unfortunately, Elaine's subsequent experiences at the inn didn't leave her with the same good feelings. These encounters took place upstairs. Mostly she experienced feelings of sadness and despair, as if a somewhat gruff and ghostly presence didn't want her to be there. On one occasion she even asked a gentleman friend to go upstairs and investigate. Interestingly, he too experienced what he described as a man's presence on the second floor.

Elaine reported that the room in which the feelings were strongest was the one in which the poet George Sterling had stayed. What makes this of interest is that Sterling was unhappy toward the end of his career and eventually committed suicide in San Francisco. The poet had also experienced considerable sadness when he lived in Carmel, including despondency over the suicide of a close friend.

After Elaine had experienced the incidents just described, a man who was very much in tune with the "spirit world" happened to stay at the inn. After spending the night, he struck up a conversation with Elaine over a morning cup of coffee. Eventually the conversation turned to the subject of the supernatural. It was then that he asked whether Elaine knew that a female ghost frequented the downstairs. When she smiled and nodded yes, he added that he had also experienced the ghostly presence of a man upstairs. Interestingly, this man was unaware of the ghosts before stopping at the inn. Judging from his comments, he got more than he bargained for when he stayed at the charming hideaway in Carmel-by-the-Sea.

A Halloween helping of hotel hauntings . . .

October 31, 1996 I have already mentioned several ghost stories connected with Monterey's magnificent old Hotel Del Monte, now the U.S. Naval Postgraduate School. As is the case with the Robert Louis Stevenson House, the stories of strange happenings just keep on coming.

Today, for example, I picked up the *Monterey County Herald* newspaper, and on the front page was an article entitled "Navy school entertains ghostly hotel guests." While I have documented several of the incidents in the article in my other books, a couple of them were new to me.

By way of introduction to these events, a quote from the navy school spokesperson who was interviewed in the article may be of interest. In reference to ghosts, this highly respected individual stated, "I've had people come tell me about the experiences they've had. Everyone I've talked to is credible. The experiences can't be explained mathematically, scientifically, or quantitatively."

I think these comments are worth pondering, as they come from someone who has worked at the facility for many years and who is definitely not the type to go looking for ghost stories. However, as an expert in the building's history, he is often sought out by people who have experienced odd occurrences there.

To continue with the *Herald* article, among the manifestations it described are the sounds of people dancing in the general vicinity of where a bridal suite was located prior to the disastrous 1924 fire, and (as related in an earlier note) where a newlywed couple lost their lives during the famed California earthquake of 1906. In addition, the article recounted a number of incidents described by the head housekeeper in charge of Herrmann Hall, the old hotel's main building. One incident she described was experienced by a maid who saw the ghostly figure of a man, thought to have been dressed in an old-fashioned fire-fighting kind of coat, walk *through* the closed door of room 319. This story is especially interesting in light of an account (reported in my book *Incredible Ghosts of Old Monterey's Hotel Del Monte*) of a fire fighter who supposedly lost his life during the 1924 conflagration.

Room 319 was also the site of an odd occurrence reported by a naval officer. The officer said that she heard strange voices coming out of the room, but upon inspection no one was there.

A long-time chef at Herrmann Hall also contributed to the article. The one odd happening that he had experienced took place in the hall's ballroom, where he saw several papers suddenly lift from a counter and fly about the room. One of the chef's co-workers had an experience of a more personal nature. According to the article, he described being "slapped" by a ghost, whereupon he left his mop and bucket where they stood and promptly quit his job!

Finally, an officer who lives in one of the "cottages" on the navy school grounds reported a number of strange happenings at her quarters. Inasmuch as Charlie Chaplin is rumored to have stayed in the cottage during his honeymoon, she likes to think that it's his presence that frequents the house.

With these accounts adding to the many mysteries of the Del Monte, I got to thinking about a couple of other articles relating to historic hotels that have appeared in the *Monterey County Herald* over the past twelve to thirteen months. The most recent was in the October 13, 1996, issue and told about Monterey's Casa Munras Garden Hotel. The main building of the "Casa" (as the establishment is known locally) dates back to the 1820s. It was the first residence in Monterey (then the capital of Alta California) to have been built outside the walls of the Spanish Presidio. It was also the first home in the area to boast an indoor fireplace. Having seen history come and go as few other buildings in California have, it somehow seems appropriate that it has a ghost.

According to the article, the Casa's ghost, who is sometimes referred to as Old Man Munras, has been held responsible for such things as dimming the upstairs lights and making a variety of strange sounds. In following up the article, I visited the structure to see what I could learn about the spirit's antics. According to the accounts that were shared with me, a cold spot has frequently been felt in the lobby of the main building in the dead of night; freshly brewed coffee has suddenly appeared, when no one was around to make it; and a distinct male presence has been felt in the main building. In addition, the "old man" has reportedly called some people by name. When they turn around, no one is there. Apparently, this occurrence takes place only in the upstairs section of the main building.

The second *Monterey County Herald* article that I mentioned appeared the day before Halloween in 1995. This article was about the Monterey Hotel and a million-dollar renovation project that was taking place there. Located in the heart of downtown Monterey, the elegant old building dates back to 1904. According to the article, a gentleman ghost who resides at the hotel has long been a part of local history. Referred to as Fred by those who work at the facility, the ghost appears to night workers as, among other things, flashes of light.

Curious about other incidents blamed on the ghost, I visited the establishment several times and talked to various employees about their experiences. As with other buildings that are said to be haunted, some agree that there is definitely a ghost, while others pooh-pooh the idea and state that they have never experienced anything out of the ordinary.

According to the "believers," the apparition is thought to be the ghost of a long-ago maintenance man who was killed on the premises. (His death is said to be associated with the elevator or its shaft.) Apparently, the spirit favors female employees, especially the night auditors. He is even reported to have "tweaked" the hair of one such worker.

While the ghost is playful around the female night auditors, he has supposedly made things uncomfortable for their male counterparts—so much so that one individual is said to have stomped out of the structure, quit his job, and refused to return to the building. A second male night auditor was reportedly unnerved by voices he heard (through a pipe that ran through his office) when he was alone in the structure. Still another male night employee was in somewhat of a panic when he reported that "the ghost" wouldn't let him leave his office, even though the door to the room was wide open! How such a thing could have occurred remains a mystery.

Finally, the individual who shared several of these accounts with me also described reports from guests who have stayed at the hotel. Among these experiences are feelings of presence, windows and blinds that open by themselves, and a television set that turned on while it was in a tightly shut antique armoire.

In closing I should add that none of the incidents at the Monterey Hotel or Casa Munras have ever created a problem for any guests. And, from all reports, both of these establishments continue to receive rave reviews from their customers.

Rambling through the Mother Lode . . .

March 23, 1997 A trip to the Gold Country, where I gave a series of talks, turned up quite a "lode" of ghostly tales, including a number of leads I'd like to try and check out at a future time. Here I'll mention just a few.

From a deputy sheriff who attended one of my talks, my wife and I learned about an allegedly haunted establishment on Highway 49. Known as the Vineyard House, the structure is located in the tiny community of Coloma, where gold was discovered in 1848. Several articles have discussed the ghosts that are connected with this building. Among the best-known tales are those that tell about the building's first owner, a man by the name of Robert Chalmers, who had the facility built in the 1870s. Many people think it is his ghost that wanders about the structure and plays tricks.

Sadly, Chalmers died a tragic death in the building's basement. According to one story, he became insane and spent the last few years of his life locked in a small room in the cellar. If this is true, I suppose we can't blame his ghost for sticking around and playing tricks. Maybe he's merely trying to relive some of the good times, before the tragedy of insanity set in.

After our visit with the deputy, my wife and I headed south through Sonora to Jamestown, where we had dinner reservations. With time to spare, we decided to mosey along the main street. As coincidence would have it, just as we were about to enter an antique shop, I bumped into an old college chum, a fraternity brother from the 1950s! He was in town to help his brother celebrate his sixtieth birthday. Later we joined him in the bar of the historic National Hotel—a delightful establishment of 1850s vintage—where we were introduced to the rest of his family, including his ninety-six-year-old mother and the hotel manager.

As our conversation jumped from subject to subject, I learned from the manager that the National Hotel has a ghost. (Perhaps I shouldn't have been too surprised, as I have already described ghosts at two other Jamestown hotels in earlier notes.) The ghost is called Flo by the hotel staff, and she has resided at "The National" since at least 1974, when the current manager took over his duties. Described as "friendly" by the people who have experienced her presence, Flo is blamed for a series of harmless pranks and odd goings-on. Even though she seems to favor the hotel's upstairs back rooms, her presence has also been both seen and felt by hotel employees in the downstairs dining room. It is here that she has been observed floating *through* the walls!

It's not only employees who have experienced Flo's presence, as several of the hotel's guests have also shared their experiences with various members of the staff. Interestingly, one of the housekeepers thinks Flo favors room 4. On more than one occasion the housekeeper has entered the room when the door has been closed and the heater turned on, only to be greeted by an icy chill.

Visitors will perhaps get an even better feeling for the old hotel and its ghosts when they read comments in the guest books that are left in each room. It is interesting to note how many of the comments deal with odd occurrences and such ghostly happenings as doors slamming, lights blinking, the contents of suitcases being dumped on the floor, and the loud laughter of women coming from the hall in the middle of the night. Of course, all of the events take place when no one is around to account for them. While some guests may find such antics annoying, most of them seem to take them in stride and can't wait to come back to experience the ambiance Flo and her friends have created in the aged building.

I might add that Flo—or perhaps a second adventuresome spirit—has recently taken to creating havoc in the kitchen. Included in the rash of unexplained happenings that have occurred in recent years are coffee dispensers that mysteriously fly out of the coffee makers, spoons and ladles that briskly swing back and forth, and pans that fall from shelves for no apparent reason.

Before taking our leave of the Gold Country (after spending the night in Sonora), my wife and I visited the historic Sierra Railroad yard. This establishment is a must for rail buffs, and is only a short distance from downtown Jamestown. Fortunately, Railtown 1897 (as the facility is popularly known) is now owned by the State of California, and has a new lease on life.

Since our visit was early on Sunday morning, few employees were around for me to talk to. However, I did find a worker who was both willing and able to chat. Not only did I gather some interesting information about the railroad—including the fact that 1997 marks its 100th birthday—but I also learned that there is a ghost (maybe two) in the old roundhouse. Unfortunately, none of the employees who have experienced the ghostly happenings work on Sunday. Regrettably, tales of the roundhouse ghost (or ghosts) will have to wait for another time.

Halloween Happenings 1997 . . .

October 31, 1997 This last week of October has turned out to be a busy ghost week for me, as I gave a couple of ghost-related talks in Monterey. The talks were sponsored by the Monterey State Historic Park and were titled "Ghosts and Mysteries of Monterey." As might be expected, these talks prompted several people to share some local ghost stories. These new tales concerned two locations I've already written about in this book, the Robert Louis Stevenson House and the old Hotel Del Monte/Naval Postgraduate School complex, together with a third structure, the historic building known as California's First Theater.

The Stevenson House tale involved the famous ghost known as the Lady in Black. The sighting was said to have taken place in the children's nursery in the late 1960s (probably 1967). It was made by a girl of sixteen who was totally unaware of any ghost stories connected with the building. Upon walking down the upstairs hall, peering into the rooms as she went, she soon arrived at the end of the hall and glanced through the barred door into the nursery. There she saw a woman in an old-fashioned black dress sitting on the bed. Thinking it was a nice touch to have a woman in costume to add to the ambiance of the room, the girl didn't think much more about it as she continued on her way and completed her tour.

It wasn't until some time later that she learned of the Lady in Black. Realizing belatedly that no one, in costume or otherwise, should have been in the locked room, she surmised that it was the Lady in Black whom she had seen.

Today the woman who made the sighting some thirty years ago is a docent for the state. She has never again seen the Lady in Black.

As to the Hotel Del Monte/Naval Postgraduate School complex, I heard about several additional happenings that are reported to have taken place in the dental clinic area of the main building (Herrmann Hall). Other than the Man in Gray presence that has been reported so many times before, one of the new images that has been seen, by two different people at different times, is that of a young girl. The first witness, a dental technician, described how he heard giggling and laughing sounds coming from one of the treatment rooms and decided to investigate. Upon looking into the room he saw a brown-haired girl of about twelve skipping and playing about the room. She was wearing a dress with colorful flowers embroidered on the front.

When this man discussed his experience with another member of the dental clinic crew (a lab technician), the second worker nodded in agreement . . . for he too had seen the girl! However, when he saw her, she was not alone. Instead, she was walking down the dental clinic hall with an older man. Interestingly, the girl matched the description given by the dental technician, and the man matched the description of the famed Man in Gray.

To top this tale off, when the first technician reported the incident to his chief petty officer, a nearby vacuum cleaner suddenly turned on and off by itself. If you're like me, you can only wonder whether the girl's ghost was letting them know that she was nearby and eavesdropping on their conversation.

With the mention of the petty officer, I'm reminded of a recent incident experienced by a second such officer. This man stated that as he walked across the empty ballroom late one night, he suddenly saw a woman dressed in a period costume, dancing by herself in the middle of the highly polished floor. The surprised officer immediately turned for a second look, only to find that the image had disappeared.

Other manifestations that are said to continue to take place at this historic facility are windows that open and close on their own, candlesticks that fall from shelves when no one is near them, cafeteria trays that are "pulled from people's hands" and fall to the floor, lights that turn on and off by themselves, and walk-in freezer doors that open and close of their own accord.

Finally, let me end this list of recent Postgraduate School happenings with a report from a current bartender. While he was in the galley behind the ballroom, he suddenly heard a thundering crash of breaking glass near where he was standing. Spinning around, he saw that a dishwasher tray full of glassware had somehow lifted from its location and fallen to the floor. Not only that, but the tray and its contents made a 180-degree turn in the process!

My last Halloween entry concerns the First Theater building. Located on the corner of Pacific and Scott Streets near Monterey's Fisherman's Wharf, this aged adobe was constructed in the mid 1840s by Jack Swan, an English sailor, as a saloon and boarding house for sailors. However, sometime between 1847 and 1850 it was converted to a makeshift theater. Because the audience paid a fee to view the performances, the structure became known as the first building in California where plays were given and admission was charged. After having served many functions over the years, today the building is once again a theater, where old-fashioned melodramas are presented.

The person who shared the First Theater stories with me has been a regular at the facility for more than a quarter of a century and has experienced a number of ghostly happenings over the years. Among the incidents she described are odd and unexplainable noises, the movement of objects, and feelings of presence. There have also been reported sightings of Jack Swan in the barroom. During performances, it is said, Jack's presence has been spotted backstage. The old sailor is even reported to have helped out actors who have forgotten their lines!

Only two structures in California are recognized by both the State and the United States Department of Commerce as haunted houses: San Diego's Whaley House (above) and San Jose's Winchester Mystery House (depicted below in a photo taken prior to the 1906 earthquake).

Located across the bay from San Diego, the Hotel del Coronado (shown here in a view circa 1890s) needs no introduction to history buffs, bons vivants, fans of classic Victorian hotels, or ghost enthusiasts. The best-known ghost at the magnificent "Del" is the beautiful Kate Morgan. The castle-like Claremont (oval) practically straddles the line between the cities of Oakland and Berkeley. The striking edifice has its own interesting stories, including tales involving ghosts.

In its day Monterey's Hotel Del Monte (shown here in a photo taken circa 1880) was known as "The Most Elegant Seaside Establishment in the World." Today the main building (inset, after having been rebuilt after a 1924 fire) is known as Herrmann Hall and is part of the United States Naval Postgraduate School.

Historic—and haunted—hotels abound in California's Gold Country. The Union Hotel (above) is located in the tiny mountain town of La Porte in Plumas County. The snow drift shown in this vintage photo is perhaps representative of the storm scene described in "Vapors of steam rose from the boot . . . ," page 29. The photo below shows the National Hotel as it appears today in the Tuolomne County community of Jamestown. Both buildings trace their histories back to Gold Rush days.

Nevada County neighbors Grass Valley and Nevada City are popular Gold Country stops along scenic Highway 49. Among their many attractions are the delightful Red Castle Inn, located high on Nevada City's Prospect Hill, and the remarkable Empire Mine State Historic Park near Grass Valley, with its imposing "Empire Cottage" (inset). Both sites have a number of ghost stories connected with them.

Upon first seeing this stately old structure in Sacramento, I was immediately struck with the thought that if there ever was a house that *should* have a ghost, this was it! It wasn't until later that I learned it was the old Governor's Mansion, and that several ghostly tales are told about it. Today it is the centerpiece of the Governor's Mansion State Historic Park.

Apparently the trip across town in 1980 didn't faze the ghosts who frequented "The Victorian" restaurant building in Red Bluff (Tehama County). Today (inset) the 100-ton structure, built circa 1900, is no longer a restaurant, and its ghosts are said to have settled down. Still, there are those who wonder about its treasure . . .

San Rafael's Falkirk Mansion was built in 1888 for Ella Nichols Parks, and it is her ghost that is said to linger at the site. Today the beautiful Queen Anne Victorian is known as the Falkirk Cultural Center and is the scene of many Marin County events.

Bodega's old Potter School (circa 1870s) in Sonoma County was used as a striking locale in Alfred Hitchcock's 1963 thriller *The Birds* (inset). Today ghosts add another dimension to the building's colorful past.

Included in the colorful history of Los Coches Adobe are tales of ghostly happenings and lost treasures. This historic structure (circa 1840s) is located slightly south of the Salinas Valley town of Soledad in Monterey County and is visible from Highway 101.

California's famous missions are among its oldest buildings, and the many tales told about them include numerous stories about ghosts. Shown here are Missions San Carlos, better known as Carmel Mission (top), San Luis Obispo (bottom), and San Antonio (opposite page).

118

According to many ghost buffs, Mission San Miguel is perhaps a better candidate for haunted happenings than any other California mission.

San Luis Obispo County's Hearst Castle is truly a California showplace. Overlooking the Pacific Ocean and filled with treasures from around the world, it is a State Historical Monument and open to the public for guided tours. If you visit the site, be sure to look carefully for the ghosts who are said to have made themselves comfortable among the priceless antiques!

STOKES
ADOBE

Built by James Stokes in the early 1840s. Scene of many dramatic incidents in the late Mexican and early American periods

Located in the heart of old Monterey, the historic Stokes Adobe has featured fine food and wine on its menu for many years, along with "spirits" of another kind. The structure was built in the 1830s, not the 1840s, as the sign suggests.

These two views of Monterey's Robert Louis Stevenson House show the aged adobe (circa 1830s) from the front (inset left) and back. The Lady in Black who haunts this historic structure is one of central California's best-known ghosts.

STEVENSON HOUSE
House where Robert Louis Stevenson lived in the latter part of 1879.

123

Fishing lore and tales of illicit activities add to the historic allure of Monterey's Cannery Row, shown here looking south (toward Fisherman's Wharf). Today the Monterey Bay Aquarium (inset) contributes to both the Row's popularity and its ghostly mystique.

The James Dean Memorial (foreground, with portion seen in inset) is located next to the Jack Ranch Cafe on a lonely stretch of San Luis Obispo County's two-lane Highway 46 (visible at left). It was near here that the legendary actor lost his life in a tragic automobile accident in 1955.

Legend states that the roar of a World War I airplane can still be heard as it flies under the arch of the famed Bixby Creek Bridge on the Big Sur coast. The Point Sur light station (inset above) is also a familiar sight to those who travel along scenic Highway One. The lightkeeper's house high atop Point Sur (inset below) is said to boast the ghost of a teenage girl.

Pacific Grove's Point Pinos Lighthouse (above) and Crescent City's Battery Point Lighthouse (below, in a photo taken circa 1913) share similarities beyond their architecture. Both are among the first lighthouses to have been built on the California coast (1850s), both are National Historic Sites, and both are said to be haunted by past lightkeepers. Like Point Sur (opposite page), the Battery Point Lighthouse is located on a prominent outcropping of rock (inset below).

127

Even though she no longer sails the seven seas, the *Queen Mary* is still a majestic sight in her Long Beach setting. Now a popular hotel and gathering place for people from far and near, the magnificent ship boasts a unique and colorful history, including tales of ghosts.

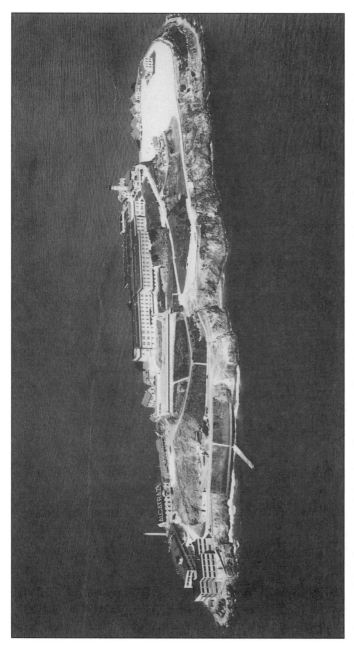

Alcatraz Island is one of the San Francisco Bay Area's most recognizable, and notorious, landmarks. Among the countless tales told about the Rock are several that feature ghostly happenings.

★ HISTORICAL ★
LANDMARK

CALIFORNIA POINT OF HISTORICAL INTEREST

During Prohibition, the San Mateo Coast was an ideal spot for rum running, bootleggers and "speakeasies," establishments which sold illegal booze to thirsty clients.

One of the most successful speakeasies of this era was "Frank's Place" on the cliffs at Moss Beach. Built by Frank Torres in 1927, "Frank's" became a popular night spot for silent film stars and politicians from the City. Mystery writer Dashiell Hammett frequented the place and used it as a setting for one of his detective stories.

The restaurant, located on the cliffs above a secluded beach was in the perfect location to benefit from the clandestine activities of Canadian rum-runners. Under cover of darkness and fog, illegal whiskey was landed on the beach, dragged up a steep cliff and loaded into waiting vehicles for transport to San Francisco. Some of the booze always found its way into the garage beneath "Frank's Place." Frank Torres used his excellent political and social connections to operate a highly successful, if illegal, business. Unlike many of the other speakeasies along the coastside, "Frank's Place" was never raided.

With the repeal of Prohibition in 1933 Frank Torres remained in the food service business as one of the most successful restaurateurs along San Mateo County's coastside. "Frank's Place" now called THE MOSS BEACH DISTILLERY still retains its spectacular views and secluded location above the ocean coves.

The Distillery also retains one of "Frank's" former customers, as well. Its resident ghost, "The Blue Lady" still haunts the premises, trying to recapture the romance and excitement of "Frank's" speakeasy years. The story of the "Blue Lady" was documented by the TV program "Unsolved Mysteries", and has been seen by millions of people around the world. Perhaps you will see her today!

As its historical marker indicates, over the years the Moss Beach Distillery building on the San Mateo County coast has catered to people from both sides of the law. At various times the structure has been known as Frank's (see photo at left, circa 1927), Frank's Place, Frank's Roadhouse, Frank's Marine View Hotel & Grill, and The Galloway Bay Inn. Thanks to a segment on the NBC TV series *Unsolved Mysteries*, today the Moss Beach Distillery is not only a popular eating and drinking establishment but a favorite destination for ghost buffs.

The birthplace of California . . .

November 9, 1997 So here I am in San Diego, the birth-place of California and home of the historic (and haunted) Whaley House. Located at 2428 San Diego Avenue in the Old Town section of the city, this picturesque antique structure was built in the mid 1850s. Described as the oldest brick building in southern California, it is listed by the United States Department of Commerce as one of only thirty "ghost houses" in America (and one of two in California, the other being the Winchester Mystery House in San Jose). As if this isn't enough to get my ghost juices flowing, nearby Coronado and its fabulous Hotel del Coronado (of 1880s vintage and boasting a colorful ghost-ly history of its own) have certainly helped to make this trip enjoyable.

In reality I'm in San Diego to attend the California Reading Association's 31st Annual Conference. But with such well-known "haunts" beckoning, I would be remiss not to make an effort to visit the two structures. So, on the night of November 8 I made my way to Coronado and its magnificent oceanfront hotel, affectionately referred to by most locals as "The Del." While I was there I wandered through the elegant edifice and chatted with several of its workers. As perhaps would be expected, they were well aware not only of its famous guests (including fourteen U.S. presidents) but also of its best-known ghost, the hauntingly beautiful—and very mysterious—Kate Morgan.

In case you're unfamiliar with this long-ago lady, Kate Morgan was a guest at The Del in 1892. She arrived alone, and, according to several reports of the time, she died alone, five days later. Most accounts indicate that she took her own life by placing a gun to her head and pulling the trigger. Her body was found, clothed in black, on a stair-well that led to the beach. Beside her was the revolver she had purchased from a nearby gun shop. Even though the death of this mysterious guest—who spent Thanksgiving alone at this world-famed resort—was discussed in newspapers throughout the nation, "The Case of the Beautiful Stranger" (as the incident became known) was soon forgotten when her death was ruled a suicide.

Then several strange happenings began to take place in the room she had occupied. Not only that, but odd occurrences were also reported in the room of a maid who had befriended Kate during her short stay at the hotel and had grown very fond of her. When Kate's body was found, the maid became very distraught. After the funeral she left the facility, never to return.

Today both of these rooms are said to be haunted, and both boast a long list of strange happenings that are associated with them. Among the reported manifestations are lights that flicker on and off, icy spots (or drafts), windows that open by themselves, curtains flowing when there are no breezes or drafts, a shaking bed, water faucets that turn on by themselves, footsteps that are heard around midnight when no one is present to account for them, and an eerie glow in one of the rooms.

Of interest here is a conversation I had with one of the establishment's workers. According to her, most, if not all, of these manifestations ceased in the late 1980s. Wondering what was significant about the late 80s, I snooped around a little more and learned that in 1989 a researcher by the name of Alan M. May uncovered some interesting facts, including information indicating that Kate Morgan had *not* killed herself! Perhaps when the truth became known (through a book he later wrote), the troubled spirit of this mysterious lady felt that she could finally move on. (Incidentally, May's delightful book, *The Legend of Kate Morgan,* is a must for anyone interested in the Hotel del Coronado and its best-known ghost.)

I hasten to add that there are those who are convinced that Kate's presence continues to linger about The Del. And, even if Kate's ghost no longer haunts its hallowed halls, there are several other ghosts who are said to frequent the facility. Among them are a long-dead caretaker who has been observed in the area of the Crown Room, where he taps the floor with his cane as he makes his rounds; an elegant lady, dressed in a costume of Victorian splendor, who has been seen "floating" across the dance floor; a sad-faced little girl who wanders the halls looking for a doll she has left behind; and a pair of youngsters (a boy and a girl) who happily run up and down the stairs between the second and third floors.

After the reading conference ended today, I made my second stop, at the Whaley House in Old Town San Diego, which is now a historical museum open to the public. A charming lady greeted me as I entered the facility and soon impressed me with her knowledge of, and obvious love for, the building. Among the many fascinating things she told me about the early history of the house was that part of it once served as the seat of justice (complete with its own courtroom) for San Diego County. Of most interest to me, however, were her tales of ghostly sightings and peculiar happenings that continue to take place both inside and outside the house.

The earliest such account dates back to the early 1850s, even before the house was built. This tale revolves around a man by the name of Yankee Jim Robinson who, early records indicate, was hanged from a tree or a crude scaffold on property that was later purchased by Thomas Whaley in 1855. Before arriving in San Diego, Yankee Jim had been something of a scoundrel in the gold fields of northern California. Included in his illegal activities were horse stealing and an alleged attempt to steal the San Diego pilot boat. After he was hanged, and after Thomas Whaley built his house, the ghost of Yankee Jim was observed walking across the upstairs sitting room to the top of the stairs.

A second set of spirits that frequent this beautifully restored home are said to be the ghosts of Thomas Whaley and his wife, Anna. They are described as having been seen in the study, the parlor, and the courtroom, and even in the yard outside.

Another active spirit that has been observed—most often by children—is the ghost of a young girl who was a friend and playmate of the Whaley children. Tragically, she had an accident in the yard of the Whaley House from which she never recovered.

These ghosts have apparently been seen by many people. Meanwhile, clairvoyants, parapsychologists, and psychics who have been invited to the structure have reportedly observed numerous other apparitions. Among their "visions" are crowded courtroom scenes where rowdy sailors, unruly bandits, and misguided prostitutes appear to be pleading their cases.

There have been many reports of more tangible manifestations as well, including accounts of heavily bolted windows opening by themselves (setting off silent alarms and bringing police to the building) and the appetizing aroma of freshly baked bread and hot apple pie in the kitchen (not to mention the distinct odors of Anna Whaley's "sweet" perfume and her husband's favorite cigars coming from various parts of the house). The list also includes the more common "ghostly" occurrences of stairs creaking, lights blinking, rocking chairs rocking, footsteps being heard, and the piano playing, all taking place when no one is around to account for them. With these being only some of the activities that are associated with this dwelling, it's easy to see why this historic structure has earned its place on the Department of Commerce's select list of "ghost houses."

Author's Note: About nine months after my visit to the Whaley House, I had an interesting telephone conversation with a guide there who had recently experienced a couple of happenings herself. The first incident she described had taken place only a few days before my call. She was leading a tour through the house, she explained, when she stopped near a china cabinet to share some information with her group. In the middle of her talk, she was suddenly "picked up" (both feet were off the floor) and moved toward the cabinet! When she was put down, she lost her balance. Before she could reach out to break her fall, she felt "a force—like a hand" catch her, preventing her from falling into the cabinet. All ten people on her tour witnessed the event, and none were able to explain how or why it happened.

The second incident had occurred one day within the past month. With the building practically empty of people, the guide went into the music room and started to play the elegant old piano (which, by the way, was used in the movie *Gone with the Wind*). While she was absorbed in her music, she suddenly felt the presence of someone beside her. Upon glancing to her side she realized that no one was there. Yet suddenly she began playing the piano like she had "never played before," as if someone was sitting next to her, helping her play.

In summing this experience up, the guide mentioned that Mrs. Whaley had been a professional musician. With this in mind, she wondered aloud whether it could have been her ghost that joined her at the piano!

A Moveable Ghost . . .

December 3, 1997 My wife and I have spent the last couple of days in and around the northern California community of Red Bluff. Our trek was occasioned by a series of talks I was scheduled to give at schools throughout Tehama County. Although ghosts were not on the itinerary, they soon made an unscheduled appearance!

The story begins with a chat we had with the reference librarian at the city library shortly after we arrived in Red Bluff. Through the librarian, we met a woman who had written a book about Tehama County. She, in turn, put us

135

in touch with a second lady who had once owned one of Red Bluff's largest Victorian homes. Upon meeting with this delightful woman at her office in the old town section of the city, my wife and I were soon engrossed in the stories she had to tell about the aged house.

Today this magnificent mansion is located on the corner of Rio and Pine Streets, near the center of old Red Bluff and its historic business district. Our informant explained that she had had the 100-ton structure jacked up and moved to this location from a different section of the city. The main reason for the move was her desire to serve alcoholic beverages to the people who frequented a restaurant (appropriately named The Victorian) that she had opened in the building. Apparently the residents of the neighborhood where the house originally stood objected to the selling of alcohol nearby, and the state denied the owner's application for a liquor license.

Undaunted by the state's decision, the building's owner promptly bought a lot across town and hired a house moving company to transport the elegant edifice to its current location. Here the owner could not only serve liquor to her customers but also proceed with plans to convert the second story of the house into a country inn.

Apparently, the neighbors who had objected to liquid "spirits" weren't overly concerned about spirits of the supernatural kind, for word often circulated around town that the stately old structure had a ghost! The spirit in question was thought to be the ghost of a previous owner who had died in the building in 1960. This lady was so thrifty that she elected to forego the comforts of electricity during her stay of more than forty years in the structure. After her death, some $40,000 was found in various nooks and crannies around the house. Many people believe that this sum was only part of the wealth that she had hidden. To some, this lends credence to the idea that it is her spirit that haunts the house and conducts a never-ending search for the rest of her lost treasure.

Other than a ghostly presence that has been felt in various rooms (most often in the upstairs back bedroom), a variety of other activities have also been reported in the building. These include the sighting of drops of blood on the kitchen floor after the floor has been mopped, the sounds of furniture being dragged across the floor of upstairs rooms, and the inexplicable movement of objects in various rooms (one of them being a large backpack-type bag, stuffed with a lamp and marker gun, that was suddenly hurled against a bedroom door!).

Several more traditional types of ghostly occurrences are also associated with the house. Included in this list are such things as the sounds of footsteps and the turning on of water faucets and television sets when the rooms are empty. A more peculiar kind of event was recorded late one night when an older man was awakened from a sound sleep by the violent shaking of his bed. In attempting to get out of the bed he found that an invisible force held him down, and that an equally invisible "cat-like presence" was rubbing against his body. Gradually, the bed ceased to shake, the force that held him began to wane, and the cat-like presence disappeared. To this day he's not sure *what* took place that night, but he does know that the event was very real. Now he is not quite so quick as he once was to discount ghosts or to pooh-pooh stories of the strange and unexplained.

As a postscript to this story, two days after meeting the building's former owner, I got to chatting with the librarian at one of the Tehama County schools where I had spoken. Lo and behold, out of the blue she mentioned The Victorian, and added that she and her husband had been guests at the grand old house before it was moved. On one occasion when everyone was downstairs talking, the distinct rumble of something being moved upstairs could be heard. Upon hearing the noise, the couple who lived there commented casually, "Don't worry about the noise—it's only the ghost!"

So, no matter where you happen to be, you never know when you're going to hear a ghost story. In this case we've even got some treasure to add a little spice to the tale. But, if you ask me, after the building's trip across town, and the amount of renovation that was done, I think there's probably a better chance of finding a ghost in the old house than a stash of money!

On the sea and in the air . . .

February 12, 1998 I don't know about you, but the more I hear about ghosts, or strange happenings with a ghostly twist, the more I wonder what ghosts are and what they are capable of doing.

For example, in *Shipwrecks and Sea Monsters of California's Central Coast,* I wrote about the dramatic last voyage of a freighter named the *Babinda.* Abandoned by her crew off the Santa Cruz County coast when fire broke out on board on March 3, 1923, the *Babinda* traveled south about 40 miles with decks ablaze and smoke billowing from her hold before slipping beneath the waves near the rocky promontory known as Point Sur. This famous graveyard of wrecked ships made such a fitting resting place for the doomed vessel that there are those who speculate that she was guided there by a ghostly crew.

A second tale of this kind takes us a bit north of Point Sur, to the awe-inspiring Bixby Creek Bridge on Monterey County's scenic south coast. Among the several ghost stories that are associated with this beautiful structure is one that involves the spirit of a daredevil pilot. According to local legend, not long after the bridge was completed in the early 1930s, a biplane of World War I vintage approached the span from the sea and proceeded to fly under the arch and up the narrow canyon! If you've ever seen the bridge, or pictures of it, you know that such a feat would have required a pilot boasting nerves of steel and complete trust in his flying machine.

Ever since, the almost suicidal flight up Bixby Canyon has been the talk of old-timers in the area. And to this day there are those who claim to still hear the unmistakable sound of the vintage aircraft as it dips under the arch of the famed bridge and flies at full throttle up the treacherous canyon.

Now, whether a ghostly crew had a hand in steering the *Babinda* to its final resting place, or whether a phantom pilot still "buzzes" the coast below the Bixby Creek Bridge, I just don't know. But certainly it's stories like these that raise questions about what ghosts can do.

All this leads me to the main subject of this note, a third incident that also occurred (at least in part) along the California coast. This well-documented event involves yet another mysterious voyage, one that to this day has not been satisfactorily explained.

As background to this story, I should mention that during World War II blimps patrolled the California coast in search of enemy submarines or other signs of hostile activity. It was for this purpose that Lieutenant Ernest D. Cody and Ensign Charles F. Adams took off from their blimp base on Treasure Island in San Francisco Bay at 6:00 a.m. on August 16, 1942.

After lifting off, the blimp (known as the L-8) passed over the Golden Gate Bridge and headed out to sea. At 7:38 a.m. radio contact was made, and the airship's position was recorded. At that time the L-8 was approximately four miles east of the Farallon Islands (about 32 miles offshore). Less than five minutes later, Lieutenant Cody radioed that they had spotted a suspicious oil slick and were going to investigate.

As the blimp approached the patch of oil, a number of vessels were in visual contact with it. Crew members watched through binoculars as the airship circled over the slick and then descended to approximately 30 feet above the water, where it dropped a smoke bomb. (According to one source the smoke bomb was a signal from the L-8's crew that they had spotted a submarine.) After dropping the smoke bomb, the blimp ascended again and eventually rose into a cloud cover, where it was lost from view. While these events were taking place at sea, a naval shore station was trying, without success, to make radio contact with the blimp. As it turned out, the message about the oil slick was the last ever received from the L-8.

That, however, doesn't mean that the blimp vanished from view. After disappearing into the clouds, the craft was next seen at around 11:00 a.m. by the pilot of a Pan American clipper. At that time the airship was cruising at about 800 feet some three miles south of the Golden Gate. A few minutes later, the L-8 was spotted again, this time by the pilot of a Navy patrol plane. According to his rather unnerving account, he was flying over the cloud cover at about the 2,000-foot level when the blimp suddenly broke through the clouds and stopped right beside his plane!

The next reports of L-8 sightings came from people on shore. The first such account came from a man on an isolated stretch of a fog-shrouded San Francisco beach. Suddenly, the giant shape of a blimp emerged from the fog less than 50 yards away and drifted toward the shore!

Fearful that the craft might be of enemy origin, the man froze in his tracks and watched as a gust of wind caught the airship and sent it in a northerly direction. Relieved to see the words U.S. NAVY printed on its side, this witness continued to watch as the cumbersome craft briefly touched down, only to again be caught by the wind and rise from the sand. Clearing the high ground behind the beach, the airship drifted over the coast highway and continued its journey inland.

One of the next people to witness the craft's odd adventure was a motorist on the coast road who saw the blimp approach the highway. Pulling his car off the pavement, he watched in awe as the L-8 rose to a height of about 100 feet and passed over the road. In the report he gave of his sighting, he stated emphatically that he saw "an officer with a white officer's cap" look out of one of the gondola's windows as the blimp cleared the shore.

By this time reports from other people who saw the rogue airship as it made its way inland were flooding local police departments and Bay Area naval bases. Among the more interesting accounts were some that came from the San Francisco Golf Club, where several golfers watched the low-flying blimp pass over the fairway and dip behind a hill. Interestingly, one caddy reported seeing a man peering out of a window in the gondola.

Other accounts of the wayward ship followed, including reports from policemen who attempted to follow the craft in their cars with sirens screaming and red lights flashing. Finally, the eerie journey came to an end when the L-8 touched down on a street in Daly City (just south of San Francisco).

The blimp was immediately surrounded by policemen, firemen, and officials from various naval stations, not to mention a crowd of curious spectators. When no one emerged from the gondola, the crew's quarters were carefully searched. Nearly everything seemed to be in order—even the pilot's locked briefcase (which was used to transport classified information) was still secure and in its proper place. However, among the things that were out of order, or at least out of the ordinary, was the fact that the gondola's door was latched in the open position (a most unusual in-flight procedure). In addition, the safety bar that was normally used to block the open door was found not to be in place. Dangling from the doorway was a microphone that was attached to outside speakers. Lying on the instrument panel was the pilot's cap—perhaps the same cap that had been seen atop an officer's head (as he peered from a gondola window) by the motorist who watched the airship drift over the coast road.

With nary a clue as to what had become of the airship's two-man crew, a thorough investigation was launched. Ship personnel who had watched the blimp circle over the oil slick testified that they hadn't see anyone fall from the craft, not to mention two people! The fact that radio contact with the crew ceased after they reported they were going to investigate the "suspicious" oil patch only added to the mystery, since the L-8's radio was working when the blimp landed.

What became of the crew, and who operated the airship after it disappeared into the clouds, has been debated for more than half a century. The fact that at least two people on the ground independently reported seeing someone peering from a gondola window as the craft made its way inland only adds to the confusion surrounding one of San Francisco's most perplexing mysteries.

So where do ghosts come in? Well, as you might expect, some people have suggested that it was a ghost who took control of the wayward blimp and guided it to its final stop. Those who support this theory point to the sighting of a figure in the gondola as proof that someone— or something—was aboard the L-8 as it traveled to its Daly City destination. Of course, the sighting could have been of one of the crew members, but in that case, what happened to him?

As with the other accounts in this section, I will leave the verdict up to you. Was it a ghost who flew the blimp from the vicinity of the Farallons to Daly City, or was it merely Mother Nature toying with the craft and blowing it hither and yon? And who was that guy in the window anyway?

By the way, the gondola of the L-8 went on to become part of one of the most storied blimps in post-World War II history, the *America,* the flagship of the famed Goodyear fleet of airships. Considered the most "splendiferous" blimp of the fleet (at least during the 1970s), the

America was built around the gondola of the L-8. Because of its colorful past, its handlers affectionately referred to it as "The Ghost Blimp."

The plane's ghost was the "soul" of a former gunner . . .

February 13, 1998 As a follow-up to yesterday's tale of the mystery surrounding the last voyage of the blimp known as the L-8, I'd like to record an account about ghostly happenings in (and around) a more glamorized warrior of the skies, the B-29. Known to some as the Superfortress, the B-29 played a dramatic role in the winding down of World War II. It was one of these huge airplanes that dropped the atomic bombs on Hiroshima and Nagasaki.

The plane I have in mind is part of the Castle Air Museum at Castle Air Force Base, in the community of Atwater (near the San Joaquin Valley town of Merced). In reality this museum display was put together from bits and pieces of numerous aircraft. The main part of the body—the hulk, if you will—was even used as a target for bomb practice at the China Lake Naval Air Station's gunnery range in the Mojave Desert. Other parts of the display airplane, including the tail section, parts of the fuselage, and much of the right wing, were salvaged from a storage yard at China Lake Naval Weapons Center, approximately 200 miles southwest of Castle Air Force Base.

Interestingly, some of the ghost stories surrounding "Raz'n Hell" (as the main part of the plane was known) can be traced to the China Lake Station. Among the happenings that were recorded at this desert location was the eerie opening and closing of a locked fuselage door (in aviation terms, "a heavy bulkhead hatch"). There was no wind or any other kind of disturbance to account for the

143

movement. And when the door was checked, its hinges were found to be broken!

Mysterious happenings continued to take place around the craft at its new home at Castle Air Force Base. Among these were feelings of presence in various parts of the plane and a ghostly figure that was spotted (on more than one occasion) in the cockpit between the pilot's and co-pilot's seats. A photograph has also turned up an eerie image in the aft gun section. A group that held a séance inside the fuselage concluded that the plane's ghost is the "soul" of a former gunner who now makes his home in the bomber's frame.

Perhaps my favorite story was reported by two master sergeants who were working on the plane's wings. Suddenly the landing lights on each wingtip flashed on. This probably could have easily been explained, except that the craft's electrical system wasn't working, and in any case the landing lights had no bulbs in them! Along these same lines, a motorist who was driving by the base one night reported seeing the running lights of the Superfortress turn on as he passed. Once again, the electrical system wasn't working at the time.

Supernatural or otherwise, there have been a number of such unexplained happenings in and around the B-29. Just ask the photographer who was on assignment to photograph the plane at night, while it was bathed in the glow of two powerful Air Force floodlights. Suddenly everything went dark, as the "always dependable" generator stopped working. Needing only a few more pictures to complete his assignment, the photographer was understandably frustrated, but his troubles were only starting. Next he discovered that the batteries on his strobe light (which worked independently of the generator) had gone out at exactly the same time. Being conscientious about his work, and prepared for most emergencies, he went to his car to get his backup batteries, only to discover they had gone dead too!

Coincidence? Perhaps. All I know is, the stories I've recorded in the past couple of days leave me no closer to figuring out what ghosts are, or what they are capable of, than when I started.

The Claremont's ghost room . . .

March 15, 1998 During a stop in Berkeley to meet with my editor, my wife and I decided to visit the historic, and still very grand, Claremont Hotel. Situated in the Oakland/Berkeley hills and boasting one of the East Bay's most prestigious addresses, this elegant castle-like structure and its surrounding grounds are billed as the Bay Area's only Resort Hotel and European Spa. In addition to its old-world atmosphere, many amenities, and breathtaking vistas of the San Francisco skyline and beyond, the Victorian-style establishment also is rumored to have a ghost.

I first heard of the ghost many years ago from a student I met whose father worked at the Claremont. With this in mind, I decided to ask the clerk at the registration desk whether, in fact, there was a ghost at the hotel.

My question brought a smile to the clerk's face. After a brief conference, he and a second clerk admitted that several odd occurrences had reportedly taken place at the Claremont. They even punched up the room number in which most of the activities are alleged to have happened, which brought to the screen a brief message indicating that the room was (or at one time had been) haunted. However, rather than discuss any of the incidents in detail, the clerks suggested that I talk to the concierge.

Unfortunately, there was no concierge on duty at the time, so I ended up talking to a bellhop instead. He readily agreed that he had heard of some strange things that had taken place in the "ghost room" over the years. Most of those who are aware of the events, he said, believe that the apparition that haunts the room is that of a little girl.

Later on, after meeting with my editor, I returned to the hotel. This time a second bellhop took me up to the ghost room, which is on the fourth floor (it was being renovated at the time). I also had a delightful chat with one of the concierges. From this visit, along with some further detective work, I learned of several happenings that are reported to have taken place in the room.

One of the most recent incidents is said to have occurred within the last couple of months (in either January or February of 1998). As the story goes, a couple approached the registration desk in the middle of the night, more than a bit ruffled, and abruptly checked out of the hotel. Apparently they had awakened from a sound sleep, both in the belief that an invisible something was hovering over their bed! Unsure as to what it was, and not being at peace with the presence, they decided that rather than share the room with an unseen thing, they would pack their belongings and seek shelter at a second site.

On another occasion, when a couple decided to check out of the ghost room, they carefully packed their things and left their bags in the room next to the door. Upon reaching the registration desk and settling their account, they asked to have their bags brought down. A few minutes later, the bellhop came down empty-handed. Their belongings, he said, were not packed yet, as things were still scattered about the room. Surprised, and more than a little concerned, the couple immediately followed the bellhop back to the room, only to find their bags open and piles of clothing (as well as other objects) neatly stacked in both the bedroom and the bathroom. Neither the bellhop nor the couple could explain what had happened. Although their things had been rearranged, the couple was relieved to discover that nothing was missing.

This episode is right in line with reports from some of the hotel's housekeepers. On more than one occasion, after cleaning the ghost room and leaving it ready for the next guests, they returned to find things amiss.

Other unexplained happenings at the Claremont include shadowy apparitions that have been seen by both guests and workers; windows that shut of their own accord; quick swishes of air when no one is there; white flashes that appear for no apparent reason; doors that rattle when the day (or night) is still; elevators that move from floor to floor when no one has called for them; and items that mysteriously disappear, only to reappear at some other place (such as an old room key that turned up at the registration desk many years after the locks had been changed). In closing, however, I hasten to add that, according to the concierge, if the Claremont does have a ghost, it most certainly is a friendly one!

"You must have seen the ghost of Father Serra . . ."

May 26, 1998 Today's mail brought a ghost story about historic Carmel Mission, the headquarters of the California mission chain and the place where its founding father, Junipero Serra, is buried.

The story comes from a local woman I will call Suzy, who saw me on television a few days ago discussing ghosts along California's central coast. Originally Suzy had called me to share several tales, but as I couldn't keep up with the details, she kindly agreed to jot down her stories and mail them to me.

The Carmel Mission incident occurred in 1995. Suzy was in the habit of visiting the historic church, and she especially liked to walk through the garden area and the small cemetery to the north of the main mission building. One day when she was at the west end of the cemetery, enjoying the peacefulness of the scene, she looked up to see a figure strolling about the grounds. Apparently a monk, the figure was cloaked in a robe and walked with his head down and his hands clasped in prayer. About his waist was a long string of wooden beads.

Caught up in the moment, and the calmness that seemed to accompany the figure, Suzy watched as the monk followed a circular path (his head bowed all the while) and entered a small shed near the entrance of the cemetery. Wishing he had stayed longer, Suzy started toward the structure, only to see an elderly gardener leave the building a few seconds after the monk entered.

Upon catching up with the gardener, Suzy asked him where the monk was, as she wanted to talk to him. The gardener was visibly confused by her question, and after a short pause he began to explain that there were no monks there, but that there were priests in the rectory on the other side of the church. Shaking her head, Suzy replied that she didn't want to see a priest, but that she would like to speak to the person who had gone into the shed he had just come out of.

Perplexed by her request, the gardener assured her that no one had been in the building but him. Then, after a moment's hesitation—and after turning a few shades paler—he continued in a somewhat shaken and hushed voice, "You must have seen the ghost of Father Serra. . . . He hasn't been seen for a while."

In closing her Carmel Mission account, Suzy admitted to feeling "a little odd," because the monk certainly wasn't your typical "misty, see-through type of ghost." She also mentioned that the monk "didn't have a face" (at least one she could see), since it was hidden by the hood that covered his head.

About all I can add to this story is that it's too bad Suzy didn't see the face of the monk-like figure. If she had, she might have been able to confirm whether or not it really was the ghost of Padre Serra—who, judging by the gardener's words, has been seen by others strolling the grounds of his beloved mission!

Grandma and Grandpa's ghosts watch over them . . .

May 26, 1998 The letter from Suzy (see previous note) also described some interesting happenings in a small, turn-of-the century dwelling in Pacific Grove. The building in question is on Monterey Avenue, a short distance from the beach, and has been owned by the family of one of Suzy's friends for many years.

As the story goes, the ghost of the current owner's grandfather (who allegedly tipped a few with John Steinbeck when the famous writer lived in a cottage nearby) has been seen in the dwelling. One such sighting took place when the current owner was away on a business trip and his wife, Suzy's friend, was alone in the house with her young daughter. Feeling uneasy, as she didn't like staying in the house when her husband wasn't there, the mother put her daughter to bed early and went to bed herself. Sometime during the night she awoke to find the figure of an older man standing in the bedroom looking at her. The look was not menacing in any way. Not knowing what to do, she hid under the sheets and prayed for him to go away. Eventually she fell asleep, and when she awoke in the morning he was gone.

One of the things that made this experience so frightening was that Suzy's friend had no idea who the man was. It wasn't until some time later, when she was looking through some of her husband's family pictures, that she saw a photograph of a man who looked familiar. Not able to remember where she had seen him, she asked her husband who he was. Her husband replied that there was no way she could have known him, as the picture was of his grandfather, who had died many years before. It was then that Suzy's friend realized that the image in the photograph was identical to the apparition she had seen in the bedroom!

On another occasion, when her husband was gone and her daughter was sick, Suzy's friend reported that upon waking up in the morning the little girl said that during the night a nice old lady had wiped her forehead. Curious as to who the visitor was, Suzy's friend showed her daughter some of her husband's family pictures. When she turned to a picture that showed her husband's grandmother, the girl exclaimed, "That's the lady who wiped my forehead!"

With these incidents being only two examples of the many times Grandma and Grandpa's ghosts have been seen (or felt), I will end this section by saying that even though Suzy's friend is still uneasy when her husband is away, she has become more accustomed to sharing the house with his grandparents, and admits that it's rather nice to have them around to watch over and protect her.

A tale of two bed and breakfast inns . . .

June 2, 1998 True to the promise in her first letter, my new pen pal Suzy (whom you met in the two preceding notes) has sent me some additional ghostly stories. Today's letter tells the tale of two bed and breakfast inns, one in Pacific Grove and one in California's Gold Country.

The first of these structures is one of the most popular of Pacific Grove's many charming inns. Located near the heart of this "last hometown" (as Pacific Grove is known to many), the establishment has a long history of housing visitors, as it became a boarding house soon after it was built in the 1880s.

The inn's best-known ghost has been seen only in the front corner room upstairs, and then only at certain times. It seems that a gentleman clothed in Victorian finery (complete with a long black waistcoat and black top hat) appears at the foot of the bed in this room when couples are being amorous! As might be expected, the occupants of the room who have witnessed this apparition also report a rather sudden loss of romantic inclinations.

No one knows for sure who the ghostly guest is, but the consensus seems to be that he is either a jealous husband who found his wife cheating on him or simply a voyeur of the supernatural kind.

Suzy's second story takes us to a bed and breakfast inn in the Gold Country community of Amador City, on California's historic Highway 49. The establishment in question dates back to the 1850s and originally housed a saloon. As was the custom during this period, the upstairs section of this Gold Rush gathering place contained rooms for the "guests" of the saloon girls.

It is one such girl that this story is about. This account comes from a clerk at the inn, who told Suzy the story when she stayed there. Long ago, the clerk related, when miners and prospectors were combing the Sierra foothills, the saloon—and its upstairs rooms—had a steady stream of customers. One patron in particular favored one saloon girl over all the others, and it wasn't long before a relationship developed. However, when the girl became pregnant with what she thought was the patron's child, he wouldn't accept that the baby was his. From that point on he refused to have anything further to do with either the girl or the child.

Nevertheless, because of her feelings for the man, the young mother loved the baby all the more, and consoled herself in the fact that if she couldn't have the father, she could at least have his child.

After the baby was born the girl continued to work at the saloon. One night when she was downstairs a fire broke out in an upstairs room. Upon hearing the commotion, and seeing the flames race from room to room, the mother ran to the staircase to try and save her child. Unfortunately, by the time she reached the steps much of the second story was engulfed in flames. When she frantically tried to climb the stairs, several of the miners stopped her from going up.

Tragically, the baby perished in the fire. Not long after that the bereft young mother (who was barely in her twenties) died of a broken heart.

As you have probably guessed, the ghost that haunts the upstairs section of the saloon (which was rebuilt after the fire, and which is now a part of the bed and breakfast inn) is said to be the spirit of the mother, who continues to search for her child. Among the manifestations that the teller of this tale described to Suzy are guests' reports of hearing a woman crying. While the sobs are very real, and the source of them has repeatedly been sought, no one has ever been able to find where they are coming from. In addition to sounds, there have also been sightings of "something" (a haze? a mist? a cloud? a form?) floating up the staircase and heading toward the area where the baby's room had been.

Perhaps the most interesting, and insightful, report comes from a man who was a guest at the inn several years ago. Upon approaching the clerk, he asked who the "saloon girl" was that he had seen in the building. Knowing there were no such ladies staying at the inn, the clerk was at a loss to explain who she was. When he asked the guest if he could describe her, the man responded that he had not paid close attention and could only say that she had been dressed in clothes of long ago, of the sort that a saloon girl might wear, and that she appeared very sad as she wandered about the premises. Since no one resembling a saloon girl (or lady of the night) was staying at the inn, both the guest and the clerk surmised that it might have been the apparition of the distraught mother that he had seen.

This brings us back to Suzy and her stay at the inn. After hearing the sad tale of the deaths of the saloon girl and her baby, she had mixed feelings about spending the night. However, after talking the matter over, she and her husband decided to stay. The night passed uneventfully, as far as ghostly sightings are concerned. However, Suzy reported that she lay awake most of the night and experienced a feeling of "immense sadness." Oh, and one other thing: although there was no sign of fire anywhere in the building, she also reported that she smelled smoke . . .

The lady lightkeepers of Point Pinos Lighthouse . . .

June 15, 1998 A third letter from Suzy (see two preceding accounts) mentioned, among other things, a feeling of presence and a touch by an unseen thing she experienced while visiting Point Pinos Lighthouse in Pacific Grove. She is not alone, for the aged lighthouse has an honored place on the list of historic sites that are said to be haunted.

Built in 1855, Point Pinos is the oldest continuously operating lighthouse on the West Coast. It also has the distinction of having been managed at different times by two lady lightkeepers, both of whom were pioneers in what was decidedly a man's world. The second of these able and strong-willed women, a widow named Emily Fish, lived at the facility from 1893 to 1914. It is her spirit that is thought to linger about the place to this day.

Several people (residents and visitors alike) have commented on the ghostly presence they have felt in the aged building. A number of docents who work at the site have also reported a variety of odd happenings, including the movement of objects in various rooms (usually upstairs). Interestingly, the living quarters, which are maintained by the Pacific Grove Museum of Natural History, have been restored to look as they did when Emily Fish lived there.

There is also a fascinating, if tragic, tale connected with the first lady lightkeeper of Point Pinos, Charlotte Layton. As the story goes, in the 1850s her husband, Charles, was part of a posse that tracked down the notorious outlaw Anastacio Garcia after he had cruelly murdered two Monterey men. During an intense siege at Garcia's hideout, three members of the posse, including Charles Layton, were killed. (Garcia escaped, but ultimately was captured in the hills near Los Angeles. Later he was hanged by a local vigilante committee in the Monterey jail.) It was upon Charles' death that Charlotte Layton took over her husband's duties—thus becoming perhaps the first female keeper of the light on the West Coast.

Author's Note: Located on Pacific Grove's "Point of Pines" at the southerly entrance of Monterey Bay, Point Pinos Lighthouse has been designated a National Historic Site. A popular tourist attraction, it is open to the public and is well worth a visit.

An unnerving night at the Winchester Mystery House . . .

August 5, 1998 In discussing San Diego's Whaley House in an earlier note, I mentioned that it is one of two structures in California that are listed as "ghost houses" by the United States Department of Commerce. This fact brings to mind the second of these buildings, the Winchester Mystery House in San Jose, and a fascinating account that writer Richard Winer shared with me about spending the night in this most unique of mansions. (Richard, as you may remember from the tale of James Dean's cursed Spyder, is the author of *The Devil's Triangle* and, with Nancy Osborn, of *Haunted Houses*.) Before I get to Richard's experience, though, let me briefly summarize the strange tale behind the Winchester House.

The story begins with a young woman named Sarah Pardee. Born in New Haven, Connecticut, in 1839, Sarah grew into a highly cultured and intelligent young lady. Petite and lovely, she mastered four languages (besides English) before she was eighteen and was a talented and much sought-after pianist.

In 1862, the belle of New Haven married William Wirt Winchester, the son of Oliver Fisher Winchester, the manufacturer of the famed Winchester Repeating Rifle. In 1866 Sarah and William lost their only child. Tragically, fifteen years later William also died.

Deeply upset by the loss of the two most important people in her life, the grieving Sarah followed the urging of a friend and decided to consult a medium. The medium told Sarah that her loved ones were being taken in revenge by the spirits of those who had been killed by the Winchester rifle. The seeress went on to say that Sarah might be able to escape the evil curses and vengeful deaths—and perhaps even gain eternal life—if she went far away and built a house on which work would never stop or be completed. The dwelling not only would be a home for herself, but would provide space for the spirits of the terrible gun's victims. So it was that Sarah came west and began an odyssey that lasted 38 years. Upon her arrival in the Santa Clara Valley in 1884, the grieving widow purchased an eight-room farmhouse on the outskirts of San Jose. She spent the remainder of her life in continuous construction of one of the most unusual houses in the world.

The result was a rambling structure boasting no fewer than 160 rooms—not counting the many rooms, towers, and turrets that were lost to the San Francisco earthquake of 1906. In constructing this elaborate edifice, Sarah never had to worry about money. At her husband's death she had inherited 20 million dollars, plus an additional income of $1,000 a day. With virtually unlimited funds at her disposal, she used only the best materials, including such fine woods as teak, cherry, rosewood, mahogany, ebony, and ash. Needless to say, she also hired the best carpenters and craftsmen she could find. These workers were a dedicated bunch who worked a variety of shifts as the ceaseless construction continued around the clock, 365 days a year.

By the time Sarah died, the mansion covered an area of about six acres. Among its multitude of fixtures are nearly 1,000 doors, 52 skylights, 3 elevators, 40 staircases, 47 fireplaces, and more than 1,250 windows containing about 10,000 panes of glass. Scattered about the house are rooms of many shapes, sizes, and functions, including at least 40 bedrooms, 6 kitchens, and 13 bathrooms.

Interestingly, the number 13 had special significance for Sarah, and she incorporated it into the master plan whenever the opportunity presented itself (and sometimes when it didn't). An example of this is the 13th bathroom, which has 13 windows (as do many of the rooms) and 13 steps that lead into it. Oh, yes, there are also 13 panels in the wall next to it.

Other uses of the number 13 found throughout the house include 13 blue and amber stones in Sarah's prized spider web window; 13 glass cupolas in the greenhouse; 13 clothes hooks in the séance room; 13 squares in each section of the ballroom floor (with 13 gas jets in the room's chandelier); 13 steps in most of the staircases (with 13 stanchions supporting many of their banisters); and 13 palm trees that line the driveway.

Incidentally, the association with the number 13 outlived Sarah herself. Her will contained 13 parts; approximately 13,000 gallons of paint were used in the building's restoration; and the Winchester Mystery House became a California Historical Landmark on the 13th of May, 1974.

Besides her obsession with the number 13, another of Sarah's peculiarities was her insistence on involving her spirit friends in the design of the house. Perhaps it was this partnership that resulted in such structural oddities as staircases that led to blank ceilings, hallways that went nowhere, cabinets that opened into blank walls, and a second-story door that led to a 20-foot drop.

Over the years, thousands of visitors have come to marvel at Sarah's mansion, but Richard Winer is the only person I know who has actually spent a night there. Along with the co-author of *Haunted Houses,* Nancy Osborn, Richard stayed in one of Sarah's favorite rooms, the Daisy Room (which gained its name from the daisies in its stained-glass windows.) It was in this room that Sarah was sleeping when the great earthquake of 1906 hit the area. Not only was she terrified by the temblor, but she was trapped in the room by a fallen beam for several hours. After she was freed, Sarah instructed her workers to seal the room off from the rest of the house. As the story goes, no one set foot in the Daisy Room for the next sixteen years, or until after Sarah's death.

It was a remark from their guide that persuaded Richard and Nancy to choose this room as the place where they would spend the night. As they were touring the house, the guide commented that in her opinion the Daisy Room was the "spookiest" place in the house. Almost as an afterthought, she added, "I wouldn't spend the night in there for anything!" Upon further prompting, the guide described how certain parts of the room got "chilly" and how she and some of the other guides got the feeling that they were "not alone" and were "being watched" when they were in the room.

That was all that Richard and Nancy needed to hear. The "spooky" Daisy Room sounded like just the place for an overnight stay in the Winchester Mystery House!

With this background, it's probably not surprising that both Richard and Nancy felt a chill upon entering the room that night in the company of the security director. This gentleman soon added to their apprehensions with a warning not to go downstairs, since if they tripped an alarm "every cop in San Jose" would converge on the house. As if that wasn't enough, before taking his leave he also warned them not to stand in front of the windows, "especially with your flashlights on." Asked to explain this remark, the security director pointed to small holes in the windows and punctured places in the walls where bullets were embedded. "Sniper fire!" he commented tersely.

With holes in the windows, bullets lodged in the walls, no electric lights on the second floor, and no furniture in the room, our intrepid ghost hunters agreed that they had certainly stayed in more comfortable quarters. But they were resolved to spend the night in the Daisy Room, and as it turned out they were "rewarded" for this decision by a number of odd experiences.

Among these, Richard told me, were the cold spots and feelings of presence that the guide had mentioned (Richard was more in tune to the cold spots, while Nancy picked up on the feelings of presence). More noteworthy, however, was an event that occurred around 2:00 a.m., after Richard had dozed off. Suddenly an excited Nancy was shaking him awake.

"Wake up! Wake up!" she cried. "Listen, do you hear it?"

"Hear what?" mumbled Richard, still half asleep.

"The music! The music! Someone's playing the piano. It's coming from somewhere down the hall."

As Richard strained to hear the music, suddenly the floor started to shake. Lasting about thirty seconds, the tremor gave both of them a pretty good shake.

After this excitement they found sleep hard to come by and stayed awake the rest of the night. During these early morning hours they experienced several other unusual things, which they discuss in their book *Haunted Houses*. (If you're interested in the Mystery House, I heartily recommend getting a copy of this book, which was originally published in 1979.) But the real "kicker" to this story, as Richard shared it with me, is what happened when dawn finally came.

As they made their way out of the house, Richard asked the first person he came to, an early arriving janitor, about the earthquake that had struck during the night and how much damage it had done.

A bit bewildered, the janitor replied that he didn't know anything about an earthquake and that he must have slept through it. Thinking that the janitor must be quite a sound sleeper, Richard proceeded to check with other people and sources, including representatives from seismograph stations throughout the state. As you've probably guessed, he was forced to conclude that—despite the thirty seconds of shaking that he and Nancy had endured in the Daisy Room—there had been no earthquakes that night in San Jose!

With this in mind, one can't help but wonder whether Sarah Winchester's spirit still lingers in the Daisy Room . . . and, on occasion, continues to relive the terrifying temblor of 1906. After all, she *was* trapped in that room; much of her house *was* destroyed by the quake; and, for a time during this frightening experience, she *was* convinced that spirits from the thousands of victims who had been killed by the Winchester rifle had come for her soul!

Author's Note: The Winchester Mystery House is open to the public (during the daytime, that is) and is located at 525 South Winchester Boulevard, San Jose.

The Governor's Mansion . . .

September 26, 1998 Here I am in Sacramento, where I'm supposed to take part in the Ninth Annual "Sacramento Reads" Festival. The problem is it's raining, and the Festival is held outside! You know what moisture does to books . . . and in this case to the thousands of book lovers who were expected to attend.

However, even though the Festival was not a success, the weekend wasn't a total washout for me. After several years of trying, I was finally able to obtain some information about ghostly happenings at the stately old Governor's Mansion on the corner of 16th and H Streets. Not only that, but I was lucky enough to have a private tour of the unrestored upstairs section, where tourists aren't usually allowed to go.

I still remember the first time I saw this building, more than twenty years ago. I remember marveling at its Victorian splendor, its towers and turrets, and its gingerbread trim. I also remember remarking that if there ever was a house that *should* have a ghost, this was it! It just had that *look* about it.

At the time I didn't know that the elegant old edifice, which was originally built for August Gallatin in 1877, had served since 1903 as the official home of thirteen California governors. (Prompted in part by his wife, Nancy, who called it a "noisy firetrap," Governor Ronald Reagan broke with tradition and moved elsewhere in 1967.) When I did learn the identity of the building (from the sign outside that I had managed to overlook on the many occasions I had passed by the structure), I tried without success to unearth any interesting (especially ghostly) tales connected with it.

Then, in 1996, a chance meeting at a book signing in Monterey introduced me to a delightful lady who turned out to be a state-employed guide at the mansion. She assured me that there were indeed some ghostly stories associated with the structure, but that it would take her some time to gather the information.

As it turned out, my current visit to Sacramento finally provided the opportunity to stop by the mansion and pick up the items she had collected for me. While I was there, I not only had the chance to tour the building, but also was able to talk with a second guide who kindly shared some insights as well as some additional ghostly information. The content of this note is taken from these sources.

I should start by noting that the only death of a "first family" member to occur in the dwelling was that of the wife of Governor Culbert Olson. Kate Olson had been ill for many months before she succumbed to a series of cerebral hemorrhages in April, 1939. This sad event is said to have taken place in the master bedroom. However, those who have reported peculiar happenings at the house are by no means convinced that it is Kate Olson's ghost that is causing them.

The most frequently repeated tales of odd occurrences at the mansion concern strange noises. Perhaps the best-known story of this kind dates back to Governor Earl Warren's regime of the 1940s and 50s. This tale was told by one of Warren's sons, who was a teenager at the time. His room was the converted servant's quarters near the top of the back stairs. One evening when he was alone in the house studying for a school exam, he heard foot-steps on the stairs and then outside his door. When he called out to see who was there, the footsteps stopped. Knowing that the aged edifice sometimes creaked with age, and that rats and mice could occasionally be heard within the walls, he wondered whether it could have been those noises that he heard. However, when the sounds started anew he was certain they were footsteps. After he called out a second time, the footsteps stopped again.

This was repeated several more times, with young Warren becoming more and more convinced that one of his brothers or sisters had sneaked into the house and was playing tricks on him. Finally, he decided to wait by his door. The next time he heard the footsteps, he would throw the door open and surprise whoever was there. But, when he again heard the sounds and threw the door open, the only one who was surprised was himself, as there was no one to be seen! Thirty years later, when he shared this story with a group of docents, he was as mystified as ever about the source of the sounds.

There have also been more recent reports of mysterious footsteps in the same general area. One such incident was experienced by a state employee. As with young Warren, when the sounds were investigated, no one was there.

Other "peculiar happenings" that have been reported at the mansion include feelings of presence (one state employee described feeling an invisible someone pass close behind them and then hearing a sigh) and the unexplained movement of certain objects (including carpenter's tools and ropes that close off certain rooms). A state park ranger who spent several nights a week in the house over a four-year period in the 1970s has described trying without success to locate the sources of strange sounds that he heard at all hours of the night.

The mansion has also been visited by psychics. Two ladies from a "psychic institute" based in the San Francisco Bay Area even claimed to have conversed with "several ghosts" as they toured the building. According to their guide, when the psychics were talking to the ghosts one of the lights hanging from the ceiling started to go in circles!

Finally, I'd like to share the comment of one lady visitor (not one of the psychics), who said that while she was in the building she was "grabbed" on the rear when no one was there. Hmmm . . . I wonder if this tells us more about the Governor's Mansion ghosts than we want to know?

> *Author's Note:* As I mentioned earlier, the Governor's Mansion is located at 16th and H Streets, near downtown Sacramento. It is open to the public for guided tours, and is well worth a stop if you visit the capital city.

The mirror smashed to smithereens . . .

October 16, 1998 Nearly two weeks ago I was put on the trail of another local "haunt" by a writer for the *Pine Cone,* a weekly newspaper in Carmel. Today I had the opportunity to speak with the building's current owner and to clear up a few facts (and learn some new ones).

The structure in question houses Carmel's popular Simpson's restaurant. Constructed in the 1920s (which makes it something of an antique by Carmel standards), it was originally used as a kind of boarding house, and it wasn't until about 1959 that the first Simpson's restaurant opened. Since then the popular eatery and bar has become a Carmel tradition, though there was a change of ownership along the way and a lengthy period during which the establishment was closed.

Reports of odd occurrences in the building date back at least to the restaurant's early years. According to the current owner, feelings of presence were so strong in the bar section of the building that some of the bartenders used to neglect their duties (such as cleaning up their quarters) after the restaurant had closed for the night because of their fear of being left alone in the bar.

At least one of the spirits that are said to haunt the facility does seem to have ties to the old days, as, on one occasion, the image of the building's first owner was reportedly spotted at the bar. However, when the bartender turned to the back bar, and then back again, this long-ago lady had disappeared! A similar report describes the image of a ghostly cook that has been seen in the kitchen.

Most of the strange happenings, however, have taken place in the dining room—and most of those at two specific tables, 9 and 10. Table 10 seems to have been the most active, as items that have been placed on the table (usually bread and relish trays)—as well as couples who have been seated there—have vanished without a trace! This activity has been witnessed by at least two busboys, with one of them becoming so unnerved that he promptly turned in his notice.

While the happenings around table 9 haven't been as numerous, one disappearing act that would be hard to follow involved a dignified gentleman in a tuxedo who was dining alone. One minute he was seated at the table, apparently enjoying himself, and the next he had inexplicably vanished!

When this event was reported by the waiter to one of the restaurant's owners, her immediate reaction was one of doubt. But when she asked him if he was pulling her leg, the waiter responded emphatically, "Honestly, I swear I saw him sitting there looking pleased with himself, and then he just wasn't there anymore!"

Apparently, most of the action around tables 9 and 10 took place in 1994 and 1995, and then things started to settle down. However, perhaps the spirits have decided to make themselves known again. It seems that one night about a month ago, when the building was empty, a mirror in an employees' bathroom mysteriously fell to the floor, smashing to "smithereens." The odd part about this is that the screw in the wall that held the mirror was still firmly in place, as were the screws on the back of the mirror and the two cords that supported it. With no apparent explanation for how the mirror fell, those who are familiar with the history of this structure aren't taking any bets that it wasn't the work of the building's ghosts.

Author's Note: The building that housed Simpson's is located on the corner of Fourth Avenue and San Carlos Street in Carmel. Since I wrote this account, the restaurant has been closed.

Frémont's soul is said to walk the night . . .

October 28, 1998 I received a call today from a local radio personality whose station had put together a special contest for Halloween. Apparently, winners will have the chance to join him in spending Halloween night at the historic, and allegedly haunted, Los Coches Adobe.

The call got me to thinking about this spooky site, which I have written about before. It also led to some new information by way of a book the radio host told me about, *It Happened in Soledad,* by Mary Beth Orser.

Located slightly south of Soledad in the Salinas Valley, Los Coches was built in the 1840s. Among its many uses over the years was that of a stage stop and inn. According to local legends, it was while it served in this capacity that it was the scene of a number of murders. It seems that during Gold Rush days the inn was operated by a "mannish" woman who sneaked into unwary travelers' rooms at night and killed them while they slept. After stealing their gold and burying it somewhere on the property, she would dispose of the bodies in an unused well.

Today the well, and the unfortunate wayfarers' remains, are covered over. If we can believe the tale, so is the gold that the murderess buried nearby!

Another account that dates back a bit earlier involves America's famed Pathfinder, John Charles Frémont. In 1846, Frémont and his soldiers are said to have camped at or near Los Coches. During their stay Frémont is rumored to have lost a number of his men to such things as desertion and illness. The loss of the men weighed heavily on their commander, and even now Frémont's soul is said to walk the night in search of them.

History lovers might enjoy knowing about two other figures of repute (or perhaps ill repute) who have been associated with Los Coches. They are notorious badman Joaquin Murrieta and his bloodthirsty sidekick, Three-

Fingered Jack, who are described as having once conducted a meeting in the adobe.

With this colorful background, combined with its age and its eerie appearance, it's little wonder that Los Coches is of interest to ghost buffs as well as treasure hunters. And, according to *It Happened in Soledad,* one modern-day incident at the site involved both an "out of the ordinary" occurrence and a treasure of sorts. As the story goes, several years ago a woman who was visiting the aged structure went into a trance. Suddenly, she began to speak in Spanish, a language she had never spoken before. Continuing to speak fluently in this unfamiliar tongue, she told her astonished listeners to go to "the foot of an old oak tree." Upon following this instruction, they found a beautiful antique ring! Where the ring came from, or who left it there, no one knows.

Hmm . . . I wonder whether, given the chance, the lady might visit Los Coches again and "channel" the exact location where the stage-stop murderess stashed her ill-gotten treasure so long ago!

Author's Note: Certainly, other accounts are told about Los Coches, such as those describing images that appear in photographs but not to the naked eye, cameras that act peculiarly in certain rooms, and the sightings of nearby campfires (accompanied by the sounds of the campers' horses), when nothing of the kind is actually there. But perhaps it's best to let these stories rest, as for me the best Los Coches accounts are about treasures rather than ghosts.

"The most horrifying house haunting in Western U.S. history . . ."

November 20, 1998 Several months ago my editor sent me an article from the *San Francisco Chronicle* describing an event in Oakland that one paranormal expert called "probably the most horrifying house haunting in Western U.S. history." Even though the incidents occurred in 1874, the reporter who wrote the story interviewed some current residents of the area who claim that strange goings-on continue to occur in the immediate vicinity of the long-ago haunting. With this in mind, I decided to pay the place a visit the next time I was in Oakland.

My chance finally came today, as I happened to be in Oakland for the annual conference of the California School Library Association. When things shut down this afternoon, I drove to the intersection of 16th and Castro Streets. It was here that the two-story mansion had stood where the "horrifying hauntings" of 1874 allegedly took place. Unfortunately, the house was torn down in the 1970s to make room for a freeway. However, according to the article in the *Chronicle,* the intersection—and a short stretch of the freeway—remain haunted to this day.

Whether or not spirits continue to linger about the site, the original haunting is perhaps one of the best-documented such events on record. It all began a little after midnight on April 24, 1874, when three men were roused from their beds by the "eerie, incessant clanging" of the doorbell. With revolvers drawn and hearts pounding, they met on the second floor and groped their way down the stairs. When they reached the first floor and the entrance to the parlor, the clanging sounds were joined by "a cacophony of thumping and crashing noises" from "throughout the house."

Suddenly a chair came sliding toward them from inside the room. Staring in amazement, the bewildered threesome stood transfixed as, on "its own volition," the chair began to move back into the parlor. Gathering their courage, the men cocked their pistols and followed the chair. Upon entering the room they were met by an even more amazing sight. As quoted from a source of the time, the men witnessed such things as chairs "marching around the room in pairs" while "the center tables danced about, ottomans rolled over and over, and the piano warped and twisted and groaned as if in great tribulation."

For two additional nights, the house and its occupants weathered some of the most bizarre happenings that had ever been reported in the San Francisco Bay Area. All seven of the dwelling's residents experienced the events. According to reporters who flocked to the scene from such faraway places as San Jose and Sacramento (remember this was in 1874), the furniture continued to carry on as if it had a life of its own. Among the antics that were reported were stuffed chairs, a wooden bureau, and ornate sofas "dancing jigs" across the floor. Reportedly, these heavy furnishings twirled so quickly in midair that "they became a blur." Not only that, but their spinning was so rapid that they made "the noise of a buzz-saw"! Many of the objects that didn't twirl banged into walls "as rapid as a flash of lightning."

Nor was the astounding behavior limited to the furniture. A twenty-pound basket of silverware "exploded all over one room," while a ninety-pound trunk "went whizzing down the stairs." The mansion's front door also got into the act, as it "blew off its heavy hinges." Not to be left out are a pair of gloves that "puffed full" as if being worn by "unseen hands."

As the activity continued, newspapers tried to outdo each other in their efforts to scoop the competition, and scores of reporters (as well as individuals from other walks of life) gathered around the house in hopes of glimpsing the "witchy spirits" creating havoc in the mansion. On one occasion, more than 500 people are said to have spent the night shivering "to the din of screams and crashes while the supposed ghosts careened through the rooms, levitating chairs with people in them."

With information such as this being printed in the newspapers, one might wonder just how gullible people were in the 1870s. Certainly the fad of spiritualism—which involved both belief in, and communication with, spirits of those who had "crossed over"—reached its peak about the time of the Oakland incidents. With this in mind, perhaps people were more apt to believe in the supernatural than they are now. Still, it wasn't only the residents of the house who experienced the ghostly goings-on, as they invited respected men from a variety of fields to come see the manifestations for themselves. Among those who reportedly took them up on their offer were such luminaries as the Assistant U.S. Treasurer and the Hawaiian consul. With notables such as these serving as witnesses, combined with the respected citizens who lived in the structure, it is difficult to pass off all of the accounts as figments of the imagination.

The hauntings culminated on April 26 in the most frightening experience of all. Contemporary accounts describe how the house was "filled with blinding light, causing some of the rooms to disappear." Emitting from the center of the light was a woman's ghost. Throwing her head back, the spirit ripped loose with "a long wild, shrill scream . . . half of fear and half of rage!" One resident who witnessed the scene wrote, "It appeared to me as the last wail of despair from the regions of hell itself."

Strangely enough, the apparition's pitiful scream brought an end to the activity at the mansion, and soon things around the house were back to normal. However, the debates about what had taken place were only beginning. Well-known and respected people from many walks of life took part in these discussions. As would be expected, some people dismissed the entire affair as an elaborate hoax. ("Elaborate" is certainly the operative word!) But there were many, not least the residents of the house, who maintained that the hauntings were very real.

More than a hundred years later, a similar difference of opinion exists about what, if anything, continues to take place at the intersection where the house once stood. The

Chronicle reporter (who researched more than 300 pages of documents in working on the story) found that there are those who pooh-pooh any tales of unusual events associated with the site. On the other hand, some neighborhood residents steadfastly maintain that "hair-raising" incidents continue to occur, some of them involving the strange behavior of their pets.

As for me, after stopping at the intersection and looking about, I can't say that I detected any supernatural vibrations. The one resident I attempted to speak with lived in the closest house to the corner (one fenced-off lot of old cars away). The occupant of this Victorian structure answered my query (through a partly opened door held by a safety chain) with a brusque "There's no ghost in this house!" and then promptly shut the door. Still, as I stood and looked out across the freeway—which some say is haunted just opposite the intersection—I couldn't help wondering what the neighborhood was like more than one hundred years ago . . . and what *really* happened there in that long-ago year of 1874.

Apparently there are those who believe such things . . .

December 8, 1998 While researching a story involving a lost treasure (as a history buff, I'm often on the track of such tales), I ran across an account of several ghost-related stories that had appeared in the *Evening Free Lance* newspaper of Hollister in 1978. Hollister is the county seat of San Benito County and is located just east of the historic town and mission of San Juan Bautista (recognizable to many as the location of a famous sequence in Alfred Hitchcock's film *Vertigo*). In its own way, each of these tales raises questions about natural versus supernatural explanations when it comes to weird events.

The first incident described in the article took place in the 1920s. It has all the makings of a class B movie, including such things as human skeletons, ghostly apparitions, lovers' jealousies, a hooded spirit who brandished "a long, gleaming knife in each hand," and even a note of warning that was signed by "the ghost of the Ku Klux Klan"! Thankfully, the local sheriff and constable were called in to investigate. After talking to several of the people involved, they concluded that the whole affair was nothing more than a plot concocted by a jealous lover who was trying to rid the area of his rival.

The article's second ghostly tale tells of the "blanketed" chief of a "vanished" tribe of Indians who once roamed the area of old San Juan. With him was the ghost of an "adventurous" vaquero (cowboy) who had died while looking for a lost cache of gold. The gold was said to be buried beneath the cabin of the man to whom the ghosts appeared. The ghosts told the man about the treasure and encouraged him to look for it. However, when he dug in the cabin's cellar, all he found were the bones of several long-dead human beings! As the account concludes, it seems to suggest that the ghost of the cabin's owner has since joined those of the Indian and the vaquero, and that the three of them continue their "restless roaming" in search of the treasure.

While this tale certainly adds to the lore of San Juan Bautista, it seems to have the earmarkings of a make-believe tale. I must admit that the article *did* mention that the cabin had been built on top of an Indian burial ground, which would certainly explain the bones. Still, the whole affair might best be ascribed to "natural" causes—in this case, the workings of someone's imagination.

The third account touched on by the newspaper (which I learned about in 1986) concerns more tangible events. The happenings took place in a house in the old section of Hollister. Built in the 1890s, the structure has weathered some of the most severe earthquakes that

171

Mother Nature has seen fit to throw at central California, including the great shake of 1906. This, as any longtime Hollister resident will tell you, is no idle boast. Located near the confluence of the San Andreas, Calaveras, Hayward, and Tres Pinos faults, Hollister has experienced so many quakes of every kind and magnitude over the years that some old-timers call it the earthquake capital of California (a title also claimed by other areas). Interestingly, the building featured in this story is said to be about twenty feet from the Calaveras Fault—a fact that may be significant in this tale.

Also of interest, especially to history buffs, is the distinguished background of the lady whose ghost is said to haunt the house. Not only were her husband and son superior court judges, but she was a professional pianist in her own right. Add to this the fact that her grandfather was Patrick Breen (the leader of the ill-fated Donner Party), and she becomes quite a colorful character. Her name was Amelia, and she died in the dwelling in 1965.

Now, Amelia *may* have something to do with the odd happenings that have taken place in this single-story structure, but others would say that it only makes sense to assume that some of these occurrences are probably the result of the multitude of temblors that have shaken the area. One five-year resident of the house admitted that because of the quakes the building's joints were "pretty loose," which caused the structure to "shake and rattle a lot." This may help to explain the unsettling movements and the multitude of strange sounds (from light "tap, tap, tappings" to the heavy "stomping" of feet) that the house has become known for.

Other odd happenings are not so easily explained (at least in terms of earthquakes), such as the cold spot in the corner of the house or the old wallpaper that suddenly rolled up after it had been wallpapered over. Then there is the antique mirror that was found early one morning in the center of the living room floor. It was a considerable distance from the wall, and would have had to pass over (or gone around) a dry sink with a pitcher in it to end up in the middle of the room. Both of these objects would have been knocked over if the mirror had merely fallen from the wall. And, oh, yes, despite its apparent flight halfway across the room, the mirror was still intact.

Every once in a while the ceiling fixtures from both the living room and the dining room would also be found on the floor. Neither were ever broken, and the screws that had held them up were always tight, so that no reason could be found for them to have come down.

Then there was the time, when the owners were eating, that a three-legged vase fell from an alcove where they kept a collection of crystal. Like the mirror and ceiling fixtures, the vase did not break, and there was no discernible reason for it to fall.

My favorite tale, however, takes us back to the living room chandelier. One day it suddenly began swaying "about a foot in either direction." Now, this certainly sounds like something that could have been caused by an earthquake, except that no one felt even the slightest tremor, and the chandelier in the dining room was perfectly still.

So, are these events the results of natural causes, or the work of spirits? I don't know the answer, but another question also occurs to me. Have you ever heard of wallpaper rolling off a wall being a sure sign that a house is haunted? Me neither . . . but apparently there are those who believe such things!

A ghostly gathering on Cannery Row . . .

February 11, 1999 Last night was a first for me, as I attended a ghostly gathering (of sorts) known as a "clearing." As it was explained to me, a clearing is an attempt to "make the energy of a building better," and to create an atmosphere that encourages the ghosts or other disruptive entities to leave.

The clearing took place at the studios of radio station KNRY, located in the Bear Flag Building on Monterey's Cannery Row. Back when the Row was booming, the structure is said to have supported a number of illegal activities, including prostitution. In recent years, however, any "illicit" goings-on seem to be of the supernatural variety. Among these happenings are such things as the unexplained movement of objects, temperature changes, feelings of presence, clocks that reset themselves, mysterious noises, and the appearance of objects in pictures that remain invisible to the naked eye. According to talkshow host Ondre Seltzer, as reported subsequently in the *Monterey County Herald*, the popular theory is that the unsettled entities might be prostitutes who were murdered back in the seamier days of Cannery Row.

Seltzer, by the way, is described by the *Herald* as a self-proclaimed expert in the paranormal who has been hunting ghosts for 15 years. It was his idea to stage a clearing at the studio and to broadcast it live (probably a radio first!).

So, on the appointed evening, after an on-air discussion of some of the events that have taken place in the structure, those of us in attendance formed a circle, held hands, and (hopefully) said or thought the right things to convince the entities that it was okay for them to leave and that they would probably be happier on the "other side." Not having picked up any vibes myself, I can't personally testify to the results. Those in charge, however (all of whom had experienced odd things in the building), seemed to have positive feelings about the session. One individual who worked at the station even claimed to have seen the ghostly image of a person hanging from the building's front balcony! I suppose that only time will tell whether the spirits were "tuned in" and did in fact move on to the next plane.

The *Herald* also reported that during the session itself, the spirits might have been captured on film. According to Seltzer, while the show was being broadcast, people were seeing "a strange glow and floating lights." Photographs taken in dark areas of the studio with a digital camera not only showed "strange lights" but revealed "a dark human figure." I, for one, saw odd lights in some of the pictures, but I failed to see the "dark human figure."

Be that as it may, perhaps the highlight of the evening for me was being treated to one of the oddest "ghostly" accounts I've ever heard. As the story goes, when a fellow who has had too much to drink leaves a certain Cannery Row night spot, he is approached by an attractive lady who plants a kiss squarely on his lips. Not only does this promptly sober the man up, but not one of the men who has been kissed has ever taken another drink!

Now, I know this tale sounds fishy, but I must say that it was shared with me by a credible fellow who was one of the clearing's main participants. He claimed to have talked to more than one of the men who have encountered the lady . . . and who swear that they've been on the wagon ever since!

Watch out for the birds . . .

February 18, 1999 Today my wife and I drove to Santa Rosa, where we are scheduled to take part in a book show. Upon arriving in this bustling Sonoma County city we realized that we still had a couple of hours of daylight left. So we decided to take Highway 12 to the coastal community of Bodega Bay (about fifteen miles away) and have a look around. Along the way we passed through the tiny inland village of Bodega. As we approached this picturesque community, an imposing structure caught our eye. Dwarfing most of the other dwellings in the town, the building looked like an oversized antique schoolhouse.

175

Upon turning off the highway to get a better look, we discovered that it was, in fact, an old school, having been built in the 1870s. Two stories high (not counting its ornate New England-type tower), the stately old structure (which has been restored at some point) was quite a sight. Taken aback by its bulk and its somewhat foreboding look—at least on this dark, rainy day—my wife made a prescient comment. "That," she exclaimed, "is a perfect place for a ghost!"

After admiring the ornate building, we continued on to Bodega Bay, where, on a whim, we stopped at the information center. When I inquired about Bodega and its aged school, I learned that the imposing edifice had served as the setting for some critical scenes in Alfred Hitchcock's classic horror film, *The Birds*. In addition to this distinction (and that of having served as a school for nearly ninety years), the building also boasts a ghost! Although the clerk didn't know a lot about the ghost, she had definitely heard talk about a young girl whose spirit haunts the place.

With my interest piqued, the clerk started a flurry of telephone calls, and before I knew it I was talking to the man who owns the building. Not at all shy when it came to talking about ghosts, the man said that at least two spirits inhabited the site, and possibly more. The best known (and most often seen) of the apparitions is the girl, who appears to be about twelve. Even though he doesn't know why she is there, or how long she has haunted the structure, he does know that according to those who have seen or communicated with her, the girl is friendly and feels at home in the building. Some surmise that she might be a former student at the school.

In addition to the building's use as a school, for many years the second floor served as a community hall. In this capacity it was the scene of numerous parties and happy gatherings. Interestingly, the sounds of such activities have been heard long after the festivities stopped, and, according to the owner, can sometimes still be heard to this day! He went on to mention other unexplained noises, including the sounds of doors opening and closing when no one is there.

Still other manifestations are visual in nature. One nationally syndicated television program visited the site and claimed to have picked up "spiritual images" in the structure. The owner himself has seen images of several people, including not only the young girl (whom more than one member of his family has encountered), but also what he describes as a male teacher or principal in "proper dress" (early-day school attire). Although he has observed the ghostly teacher in various parts of the building, the most obvious sightings have been in front of a window and in front of the chalkboard.

If you'd like to visit the site, just head for Bodega (not to be confused with the coastal community of Bodega Bay) and look for the biggest building in town. Old-timers know the structure best as Potter School, as it was built on land donated by Samuel Potter, who was sheriff of Sonoma County. If the old-timers feel like talking, they may even tell you about the ghost of an Irish lady who is also said to have frequented the site.

Happy hunting, and—oh, yes, be sure to watch out for the birds!

Petaluma poltergeists . . .

March 12, 1999 As I jot these notes down, it's early in the morning and I'm sitting in my room at The Inn at the Tides overlooking Bodega Bay. Yesterday was somewhat of a unique experience for me, as even though I've written a half-dozen books about ghosts, I've never spent a day seeking out such accounts. But with my wife attending a conference in Bodega Bay, I decided that this would be a good time to follow up some leads on possible hauntings I had heard about.

My first stop was the inland community of Petaluma, where I visited an inn I'd learned about previously in a search of the clipping file at the town's public library. Inasmuch as the owners would prefer that their establishment not be linked to a ghost, let me simply describe it by saying that the building was constructed in the early 1900s and was once the home of a very prominent Petaluma man. The spirit that allegedly haunts the site is thought to be the man's wife. Why she has chosen to return to the structure is unknown, but some have suggested that she was too fond of the house to leave its comfortable surroundings. The current owners also wonder whether she might be hanging around to keep an eye on things and to make sure that her beloved house is being taken care of.

While the owner I talked to was hesitant to describe in detail all that has taken place, he admitted that the building does have some peculiarities. Among them are an abundance of strange noises that have repeatedly been heard. Feelings of presence are also quite common, as evidenced by the comments in a journal the owners provide for guests to write in.

Interestingly, the lady ghost appears to prefer men, as it is usually they who report feeling her presence. One East Coast visitor who was staying in her room (where most of the activity seems to take place) told one of the owners that the inn's cat had jumped on his bed in the middle of the night. The owner replied that such a thing was impossible, as the cat had spent the entire night in the bedroom he shares with his wife. The guest then told about hearing female voices in his room during the night. Although he couldn't see them, or distinguish what they were saying, he was certain that two women were in his room carrying on a conversation.

Cold spots and cool sensations, as well as a handful of other traditional sorts of ghostly occurrences, are also said to be associated with the house. Fortunately for the owners (and their guests), the spirit who haunts the building seems to be friendly. Even though one couple did check out in the middle of the night, in most cases the ghost adds nothing more than an interesting ambiance to the delightful dwelling.

Later in the afternoon, after a trip to San Rafael (see next note), I followed up on a lead I'd uncovered through the Petaluma Historical Museum and telephoned a woman whom I'll call Alice. After asking a number of questions, and apparently satisfying herself that I wasn't some kind of kook, Alice kindly invited me to her house.

As it turned out, Alice proved to be a charming lady known to just about everybody in town. The building she told me about (not her present home) was built around the turn of the century and was known to be haunted long before she moved in. In fact, with a twinkle in her eye, Alice said that the history of the house—including its ghosts—is part of what prompted her to buy the place.

Among the apparitions that have been most often seen in the structure are a woman in Victorian finery who sports a stylish Gibson hairdo and a cat that, for some reason, favors the upstairs bathroom. Even though both ghosts have been seen on numerous occasions, they have never been sighted together. The woman's ghostly image usually is observed standing at a corner window in the downstairs living room. She is always looking across the yard, or perhaps down the street, as if she is waiting for someone to appear.

As for the cat, no one knows why it hangs out in the upstairs bathroom, but its presence has been reported by more than one guest. One lady who knew nothing about the building's past reported that as she was sitting on the toilet she felt a cat rubbing against her legs. Upon looking

179

down, she was astonished to see that there was no cat there! A second visitor opened the bathroom door to use the facility, only to see a cat come bounding out. She watched the cat run across the hall and into a bedroom. When she went downstairs, she told the owner that the cat that had been locked in the bathroom was now across the hall. The owner replied that no one in the house kept a cat, and that there certainly should be no such animal anywhere in the building. Hurrying upstairs, they searched the bedroom, but could find no sign of a cat.

In addition to these apparitions, Alice indicated that there was an odd coldness in certain parts of the house. She also said that some people who came to visit, and who were unfamiliar with the structure's history, reported uncomfortable feelings in various locations. "They weren't scared, mind you," Alice was quick to add. "It was more of an uneasiness because they didn't understand what the feelings were." Other evidence of possible hauntings was furnished by investigators from a nearby college, who claimed that—with the aid of electronic instruments— they had detected the ghosts of at least two people who resided there.

Through this all Alice continued to live in the house, and the longer she was there the more comfortable she felt with her supernatural friends—so much so that when an acquaintance and his wife took it upon themselves to rid the dwelling of ghosts, Alice became enraged and ordered them out. To date, Alice told me, she still owns the building, and as far she is concerned the ghosts can stay as long as they want.

I learned of a third Petaluma haunting through another contact I had made at the Historical Museum. The man I telephoned was quite friendly, and we had a delightful chat. He had learned the story from a couple who had since passed away, and he willingly shared it with me.

The tale begins in San Francisco, where the couple in question lived in a picturesque Victorian house. They had many friends in the city and did a lot of entertaining. They were also very knowledgeable about antiques and had an extensive collection that they used both on an everyday basis and for entertaining. Guests in their home were often amazed by the elaborate table settings and the beautiful antique china and silver that they used with their meals.

If this wasn't enough to make their gatherings special, the fact that they shared their house with a ghost certainly was! Judging from their encounters with their phantom friend, the ghost was a young lady of about twelve or thirteen. Among the odd things about this apparition was that she wore heavy boots (or possibly old-fashioned shoes with heavy heels). They could often hear her "clumping around" the second floor of their three-story Victorian when they were downstairs. A portion of the second-floor hall was also cold when they walked through it.

It wasn't only the Victorian's owners who experienced the ghost. One example took place during an evening when they were entertaining. After a time one of the guests went upstairs to use the second-floor bathroom. Soon she came running down the stairs, screaming! Not stopping to tell anyone what had happened, she ran out the door and never returned. Later, through a third party, the couple learned that she had become "unnerved" upon encountering a ghostly presence upstairs.

With the preceding information serving as background, the saga now shifts to Petaluma. When the couple retired in the mid 1970s, they sold their San Francisco Victorian and moved to this charming Sonoma County community. Upon their arrival they continued their love affair with antiques and opened a shop. However, after a time they tired of being tied down, and decided to purchase a ranch-style home on the outskirts of town that had a large outbuilding in its backyard. They converted the backyard structure to a shop of sorts and continued to deal in antiques.

The strange thing was, having moved far from San Francisco, the couple were *still* not free of their ghost! Apparently, the young lady who had haunted their house in the city had followed them to Petaluma and made herself at home in their new quarters. The couple weren't bothered in the least by their new boarder, but their dog (a large animal that resembled a husky) wasn't so sure. Things were fine when the couple first moved in, but after the apparition staked a claim to one of the back rooms the dog began acting peculiar. Ordinarily the animal was friendly and gentle—a "mellow fellow," as the man who told me this tale described him—but after the ghost checked in, the dog would cower against the opposite wall whenever it had to pass this particular room. With its hair standing on end, it would whimper and whine, and sometimes growl. As you might guess, the back room was the only area in the house where the dog reacted in this way.

So, my little spirit safari turned up an abundance of stories of Petaluma poltergeists. But there was still more to this unusual day, as I describe in the next note.

She sensed that the image was the ghost of Ella Parks . . .

March 12, 1999 In between the Petaluma stops described in the preceding note, I took Highway 101 south to the Marin County community of San Rafael. I'd heard about a haunted house there that I wanted to check out.

The building in question is the Falkirk Mansion, now known as the Falkirk Cultural Center. Haunted or not, upon first seeing this magnificent old edifice I knew it was worth a visit. Built in 1888 and described as a Queen Anne Victorian, the mansion has a stately elegance that is enhanced by its distinctive roofline (complete with gables, chimneys, and bays) and its park-like grounds.

The mansion became known as Falkirk after it was bought by the City of San Rafael in 1972. The name comes from the city in Scotland where the structure's second owner, Robert Dollar, was born. Founder of the Dollar Steamship Line (later to become the American President line), Dollar had bought the dwelling shortly after the turn of the century, and it remained in the Dollar family for many years. In 1972 it was listed in the National Register of Historic Places as the Dollar Mansion.

Although Dollar's name came to be associated with the site, credit for the building of this San Rafael "dream house" goes to the structure's original owner, Ella Nichols Parks. It was she who commissioned the well-known architect Clinton Day to build the mansion as a country estate. After it was completed, Ella lived there until her death in 1905. As you might guess, it is her spirit that is said to haunt the site.

After making some inquiries concerning stories of ghostly happenings at Falkirk (and, I must say, being somewhat persistent), I was eventually given a stack of material to go through. In it I uncovered a detailed description, recorded in October of 1998, of a vivid experience that took place in November, 1995. An administrator was working alone in the building late one night, trying to meet an important deadline, when she began hearing strange noises coming from the hallway on the second floor. After a short time, the sounds ceased. Attempting to convince herself that they had merely been caused by the wind, she tried to go back to work.

About twenty minutes later, the noises started again. This time she knew it wasn't the wind, as a quick check had told her the night was still. It was then she decided that—deadline or not—it was time for her to leave!

Convinced that "something wasn't right," the administrator hurriedly gathered her things and turned off the lights. As she made her way through the darkened house and started down the main staircase, she was startled to see a ghostly figure hurrying down the stairs ahead of her!

Upon sensing that the image was the ghost of Ella Parks, the administrator felt a sudden feeling of relief sweep over her. The spirit "didn't seem like anything evil," she reported. In fact, "it felt kind of friendly." She did admit, however, that because the event was "supernatural," it was also "kind of nerve-wracking."

The administrator, as well as several members of the Marin Heritage group (who were instrumental in helping to preserve the mansion), agree that the ghost that lingers at the site is the spirit of Ella Parks. They also agree that her presence is most often detected on the main staircase. Another location that seems to be quite "active" is the hall near Ella's bedroom.

Most of those who are aware of Ella's presence think that she likes what's going on in her house. Perhaps with tongue in cheek, some have suggested that her spirit may be sticking around to be of assistance in case any "supernatural" help is needed in bringing the grand old edifice back to its former elegance!

The wizard glowed in the dark . . .

March 15, 1999 This evening I received a call from a man in Orange County describing a rather odd event that took place along the Big Sur coast back in 1989 or 1990. Known the world round for its scenic beauty, Big Sur was also a magnet for "counterculture" types back in the 1960s—a fact that may or may not have some relevance to the caller's experience.

The incident occurred as the man, whom I will call Frank, was driving north with a friend up Monterey County's cliff-clinging Highway One. About ten o'clock at night, when they were still many miles south of Carmel, they suddenly saw a mysterious white light in the road ahead of them. At first glance they thought the object was a car coming toward them. As they got closer, however, they could tell that it was definitely not a car.

As they drew abreast of the light, they saw a man with a long white beard (reaching to his waist) walking beside the road. The man was dressed in a light-colored robe "similar to a monk's habit," and he was holding a staff "like a shepherd's, complete with a hook at its end." His hair was also long and white, and he had sandals on his feet. Strangest of all, Frank, who was in the passenger seat, told of "a strange white light" that seemed to emerge from him, almost as if he "glowed in the dark." Frank compared the figure's striking appearance to that of an "old wizard," saying that he reminded him of "Merlin the magician." As Frank turned and watched in awe, the old fellow continued to glow until the car rounded a bend and he was lost from view.

Although Frank often wondered about what he and his partner saw that night, he chose not to share his experience with a lot of people because of the raised eyebrows and looks of disdain that his story caused. Recently, however, he saw a television program involving a ghost from the Chicago area that "glowed." Reminded of his Big Sur experience, he started making phone calls and visiting bookstores that specialized in "weird things." He also browsed the Internet, where he learned of my book *Incredible Ghosts of the Big Sur Coast*. After ordering a copy and failing to see any tales of wizard-like men who glowed in the dark, he called me to find out whether I had heard any such stories since the book was published.

Unfortunately, Frank's account was new to me, and even though the Big Sur coast is filled with mystery and a sense of magic, I couldn't answer his question of who the man might be. Who knows, maybe he was a holdover from the 1960s, making a pilgrimage to a time that is no more. After all, one of the great gurus of that time once holed up in a cabin not far from where the "wizard" was seen and at a later date—in one frantic ten-day binge—cranked out a book that immortalized the area to those of his kind. The book, of course, was *Big Sur,* and its author was none other than Jack Kerouac, the father of the Beat Generation.

Of course, that doesn't explain why the man glowed . . .

A patch of purple violets . . .

April 18, 1999 Today I attended Monterey's Third Annual Independent Booksellers Book Festival. While I was busily signing and selling books, I got to talking with a lady who had lived for many years in the tiny community of Lockwood, in southern Monterey County. As we compared notes about people, places and stories that we knew, one name that kept coming up was that of a fellow I will call Brother Anthony, of Mission San Antonio (a few miles northeast of the Lockwood/Jolon area). In turn, that connection got us talking about a sad but extremely touching tale I had heard from Brother Anthony about a local family and the death of their daughter. Even though the story is not about ghosts, I think you'll agree that it somehow seems to fit the subject matter of this book.

Brother Anthony had served at Mission San Antonio for more than twenty years when I talked to him in the mid 1970s. One of the few missions that is still in its rural setting, San Antonio is also one of only five of the original twenty-one missions that are currently controlled by Padre Junipero Serra's order of Franciscans.

The story I heard from Brother Anthony concerns a girl from Lockwood whom I will call Emily. At the age of seven, Emily became gravely ill. Many experts were consulted, but it was soon apparent that her illness was incurable and that she had only a short time to live.

The course of the illness was sufficiently predictable that the girls' parents were told what to expect, practically down to the day. After being given some medications to help along the way, the couple took their daughter home and tried to make her last days as comfortable as possible.

Emily, it appears, loved Mission San Antonio, and after becoming ill she often asked her mother to take her there. It seems that it was cool inside the church, and Emily didn't seem to hurt quite so much when she was there. It was during one of these visits that Emily asked her mother if she was going to die. The mother tearfully acknowledged that she was, and explained that she would soon be going to a much more beautiful place. Upon accepting the news, Emily asked her mother if she could be buried at the mission. Seeing no reason why not, the mother promised that she would.

Not long after this conversation, Emily slipped into a coma. According to the doctors, she would be dead in perhaps twelve days, and no more than fourteen. With time growing short, her mother started to arrange for her burial. It was then that she learned that the mission officials would not grant permission to bury her daughter there. Among their reasons was that they didn't want the mission to become a cemetery. With a graveyard in Lockwood, and another in King City about twenty-five miles away, they knew there were other burial sites nearby.

That should have ended the matter, but Emily's mother refused to take no for an answer. For the next two weeks she called one church official after another, but when she succeeded in reaching them the answer was always no.

Meanwhile, Emily clung to life. Finally, on the twenty-ninth day—more than two weeks after the doctors had predicted she would die—Emily's mother received permission for her daughter to be buried at the mission. Emily died peacefully the very next day.

Now, this was already a touching story, but Brother Anthony wasn't through. After Emily was buried in the corner of the mission's inner court, he explained, a patch of wild purple violets began to grow on her grave. For many years, her grave was the only place in the court where they grew, and they continue to bloom every year. Interestingly, no soil or seeds were brought in from the outside, and the inner court is off limits to visitors.

My interview with Brother Anthony concluded at this point, but I learned a fascinating postscript to this story in an article about him that was published ten years after our conversation. The article included Brother Anthony's tale of the purple violets, but with a new twist. According to Brother Anthony, one day when he was walking by Emily's grave (approximately two years after I had met with him), he noticed that a patch of *white* violets had appeared there.

A short time later, he learned of the death of Emily's mother. As you've probably guessed, in thinking back to when he had first noticed the white violets, Brother Anthony realized that it was on the very day that Emily's mother had died!

Mysterious goings-on at Camp Pendleton . . .

June 4, 1999 While recording the receipts for the books I sold following a school talk in the Fort Ord area, I found a note clipped to one of the checks. The note read:

> Mr. Reinstedt,
> I have enjoyed every one of your books. I "ran into" a ghost the first day of docent training for the Rancho Santa Margarita y Las Flores in San Diego [County]. The two ghosts were happy to follow me through my docent career. I look forward to reading your new book.

Naturally, I couldn't let such a nice note go unanswered, so I gave the writer (whom I will call Toni) a call. Our conversation led to a discussion of her ghostly encounters, and to an account she said she would write about her experiences. But, before I get to her story, I'd like to briefly touch on the area where the incidents took place.

Rancho Santa Margarita y Las Flores dates back to California's mission period. The name of the rancho was taken from the surrounding valley and dates back to 1769. It was on July 20 of that year—the feast day of St. Margaret of Antioch—that Father Juan Crespi of the Portola expedition stopped to record the event as they passed through the valley.

Later the area became part of the Mission San Luis Rey holdings, and still later it became a rancho. In 1942 the U.S. Marine Corps purchased the property. It has served as a marine base ever since.

No one knows for sure when the first structure was built on the site of the existing ranch house, but we do know that there was a building there, or close by, as early as 1827. Rumor has it that over the years this structure has been added to many times. Today it is the home of the commanding general of Camp Pendleton.

It is this house, along with its nearby bunkhouse, that Toni's account tells about. Her initial experience was in the bunkhouse on her first day of docent training in 1995. Curious about the rooms in the bunkhouse, she was disappointed to find them all locked. When a marine who was assigned to the area saw her try the door to the tack room, he told her it was okay to open it and go in. She explained that all the doors were locked, whereupon he apologized and said he would go get the keys.

As the helpful marine left to fetch the keys, Toni tried the door again, but it still wouldn't budge. She was trying to peek through the window when suddenly the door opened by itself! Surprised, and more than a little confused, she nevertheless entered the room.

Upon crossing the threshold, Toni was met by a blast of hot air, a truly odd sensation considering that it was a cool, rainy day in late October. Reasoning that someone had forgotten to turn down the thermostat, she continued on into the room. She soon had to abandon her thermostat theory, as once she passed through the barrier of heat the temperature in the room became quite comfortable. With things apparently back to normal, Toni became engrossed in looking at the artifacts displayed in the room. Suddenly, a movement caught her eye. When she glanced toward the door (where the movement had been), the room became icy cold! Feeling her hair standing on end, Toni ran from the room.

Upon reaching the veranda, Toni saw no one about. However, she was soon joined by the marine who had gone to get the keys, accompanied by a fellow docent. Neither could explain the strange sensations Toni had experienced, or how the door had opened by itself.

After her bunkhouse experience Toni was all the more curious about the ranch house. With odd occurrences very much on her mind, she asked the senior docents whether the house was haunted. "Why do you ask?" they wanted to know. In response Toni told them about her experience in the bunkhouse. At that point the docents, somewhat grudgingly, admitted that some of the residents of the house had mentioned strange happenings. They hastened to add, however, that the incidents didn't occur very often.

With this background Toni began collecting stories pertaining to the ranch house. By December (1995) she had gathered dozens of accounts, with many of them revolving around a ghost named Yisadora. Yisadora was the sister of Andres and Pio Pico (who acquired the rancho in 1841), and the wife of John Forster (who purchased the property from Pio in 1864). Most of the ghostly incidents that pertained to Yisadora took place in or around the room she had once occupied. Perhaps the most obvious of these incidents were the strange and unexplained noises that came from her room.

Strange sounds were also heard in the attic above the room. Interestingly, there are stories that, on occasion, Yisadora would lock her unmarried maids in the attic in an effort to save their virtue. A lady and her baby are also reported to have died of heat exhaustion while they were locked in the attic.

Apart from collecting tales like these, Toni soon had other experiences of her own to relate. That same year a new commanding general and his family began allowing groups to tour the ranch house at least twice a week. During these tours, and at other functions, several odd occurrences were noted by some of the docents, as well as by two marine officers whose duties included caretaking the facility.

These happenings involved such things as displays in certain rooms being moved or altered when no one was in the rooms. Among the most obvious were leather boots (worn by the docents as part of their period costumes) that were often found turned around when the officers made their checks. Another frequent happening involved a curtain that was found draped over a cradle. The cradle had been placed in front of a window, as if a caring ghost wanted to be sure its occupant had plenty of cool air during the area's hot summer nights. (Could this have anything to do with the baby that was reported to have died of heat exhaustion in the attic?)

Other strange happenings that are associated with the house include pictures that are removed from the walls, only to be found intact on the floor (on one occasion a picture was found two rooms away); the appearance of something white, followed by a maze of bright colors, moving from one room to another; and an occasional whiff of horses in certain parts of the house (further

191

checking revealed that a stable had once been located in the area).

One evening in the middle of December, Toni volunteered to serve at a private party attended by local dignitaries, including retired military personnel and local politicians. The room she was assigned to was called the President's Room because of a comment made by President Franklin Delano Roosevelt when he toured the building in 1942.

Upon reporting to her post, Toni walked around the room to familiarize herself with the objects in it. Along the way she smoothed out the bed covers, fluffed up the pillow, and conscientiously closed the curtains. However, when she stood back to get an overall view of the room, she realized that the curtains were open again, while the bed covers and pillow were once again as wrinkled as they had been before! As Toni stared at the bed, trying to figure out how to make it look more presentable, she suddenly noticed the shape of a body that appeared to be imprinted on it. It was almost as if a tall person was lying there! But, phantom body or not, time was running out before the visitors arrived, and Toni was getting more and more anxious to finish straightening the room.

At this point Toni sought help from a second docent. This lady, too, saw the ghostly imprint of a person on the bed—except that by then the body had shifted, and seemed to be sitting up and leaning against the backboard! Toni's companion could clearly see "his" legs and feet as they stretched partway down the bed.

With neither of them able to remove the indentation, Toni decided that all she could do was joke about the image and tell guests that she simply couldn't get the ghost to leave! Interestingly, all who visited the room claimed to be able to see the image, and throughout the night Toni reported that she could feel the man's presence.

Late in the evening, Toni returned to the room after a break. Upon opening the door—albeit a bit carefully—she came upon the general's wife, who was telling a group of guests about the latest ghostly happenings that had taken place in the room—the last of which had occurred a mere two days before the tour!

One of the incidents involved a marine whose duties included taking care of the facility. One day when he was making his rounds he noticed that a pillow that belonged in one of the wingback chairs was out of place. Taking the pillow from a second chair, he proceeded to fluff it up. He was about to put it in its proper place when he was suddenly knocked out of the way by an unseen force! As he was knocked aside, he heard a "stomp on the floor," as if someone was putting his feet down in an effort to get up from a chair. With that he threw the pillow into the wingback where it belonged and ran from the room in search of a second marine who was also on the grounds.

It was after the general's wife had left the room that Toni experienced one of her most memorable happenings. Several people were in the room at the time. After telling them about the furnishings and some of the people who had stayed in the room, she related a few of the building's ghost stories. Upon finishing her tales she playfully pointed to the imprint on the bed and said that one of the ghosts had even been in the room all night! Becoming a bit more serious, she added, "That is, if you believe in such things."

At that exact moment, the light on the chest of drawers flickered on and off about six times!

If the intention behind this display was to encourage people to exit the room, it certainly worked. Never, Toni said, had she seen "so many grown men and women move so fast!" She also admitted to having been one of them!

Later, upon getting up her nerve, Toni returned to the room and checked the light. From all indications it appeared to be in good working order. Perhaps of even greater interest, after checking the light she glanced around the room and saw that not only were the curtains closed, but there was no imprint on the bed—"not even a wrinkle!"

As a footnote to Toni's account, I'd like to share one last incident that she learned about from one of the marines who worked at the ranch house on a regular basis. During a long weekend when the family was away, he was making his rounds when he came to the double doors leading to the main part of the house. For some reason the doors were locked, even though they had been open the last time he had made his rounds. What made this all the more surprising was that the doors had to be secured with steel rods that slid into slots in the floor and ceiling. They could only be locked from the inside.

Thinking that the rods might be only partially in place, the marine pushed against the doors with all his might, but they didn't budge. Eventually he went in search of his partner, thinking that perhaps it was he who had gone through the private quarters and locked the doors from the inside.

When he found his fellow marine on the other side of the house, his partner said that he had not even been in the private quarters and certainly had not locked the doors. At this point the two of them returned to the doors, only to find them open, with splintered wood around the holes where the rods had fit!

Neither marine could explain what had happened, but they, like Toni and several other people who are familiar with the ranch house, are quick to admit that *something* mysterious is going on in Camp Pendleton's aged adobe!

Menlo Park's Coleman Mansion . . .

June 11, 1999 I've already related how I learned about the house in Bodega that served as a school for many years before "starring" in Alfred Hitchcock's film *The*

Birds. Well, not long after, I heard about a second eye-catching building of Victorian vintage that also served as a school, has become known for its ghosts, and was the site of a major motion picture. The film was a Disney production called *Escape to Witch Mountain,* and the building is the Coleman Mansion in Menlo Park.

Anxious to check out the building, I decided to work in a visit during a trip to San Francisco with my wife. So it was that we stopped by the stately structure on Menlo Park's Peninsula Way.

Built in the 1880s, the impressive main building is described as probably the oldest and largest surviving Victorian residence on the lower San Francisco Peninsula. Designed by internationally known architect Augustus Laver, it is considered an excellent example of country estates of the Italianate Victorian style.

Accounts differ concerning who had the house built, but the one I like the best suggests it was San Mateo County Assemblyman James Coleman who oversaw the project. As legend has it, the mansion was to be a wedding gift for his bride. Unfortunately, Carmelita, his young and talented wife, was killed in a tragic accident shortly before the structure was completed. With the loss of his beautiful wife, Coleman also lost interest in the house. Supposedly he never set foot in it again, and it sat vacant for many years.

Left to the elements, the mansion began to take on a look that was both forlorn and foreboding. Soon stories began to circulate about it. Among them were tales that said the ghost of Carmelita had been seen peering out of the windows and wandering through the empty halls. Locals began calling the place "the Haunted House."

With such an irresistible attraction nearby, it was not long before students at Stanford University got into the act. Certain fraternities, it is said, began testing the mettle of their pledges by requiring them to spend the night in the spooky structure.

Over the years, the landmark building changed hands on more than one occasion, and various people tried to occupy it. But misfortune seemed to follow each of the owners, and those who tried to live there never lasted for long. In 1906 a young woman was even reported to have died in the dwelling.

In 1925, though, the house began to take on a new life. It was then that the founders of the Peninsula School for Creative Learning acquired the property. However, as they were soon to learn, they had also acquired a ghost! Yes, it seems that Carmelita went along with the deal. Several decades later people were still talking about the many odd occurrences that took place in the structure, among them the sightings of a wraithlike woman who appeared to come and go.

Other accounts told of mysterious shimmering lights, usually obedient pets that balked at going into the building, and unexplained footsteps that were heard throughout the structure. Perhaps the best-known incident involving footsteps was reported by a caretaker who was sleeping in the house. Along about 3 a.m. he was awakened by the sounds. Even though he was terrified by the steps, he forced himself to follow them and attempt to find their source.

As he climbed the stairs leading to the second floor, the sounds grew louder and louder. Finally, as he reached the landing, the door to the room from which the footsteps came mysteriously opened. Summoning all of his courage, he entered the room . . . only to watch the door close behind him! Now that he was at the source of the sounds, the house suddenly grew silent. And, as he nervously glanced around the room, he realized it was empty!

Another caretaker (or maybe it was a custodian) told of "feeling the presence" of Carmelita on numerous occasions. Although she felt certain it was Carmelita's ghost, she was never able to see her.

Those who did see the apparition often described it as being dressed in green. At times, the entire image was said to have a greenish tint to it. It's not only adults who have seen the ghost, as generations of children are also reported to have glimpsed the phantom figure. In fact, on more than one occasion, a group of some fifteen or more students witnessed the apparition.

The children, like the adults, are not afraid of the ghost, as no one has ever been hurt by it. One official even looks upon the apparition as being benevolent in nature.

If these incidents have whetted your appetite about the Coleman Mansion's ghost, you might want to get a copy of Antoinette May's book *Haunted Houses and Wandering Ghosts of California*. In it she devotes several pages to the grand old Victorian, and even includes information on a second and third ghost that may also haunt the site!

The pianist's head came crashing down on the keyboard . . .

June 12, 1999 From the Coleman Mansion in Menlo Park (see preceding note), my wife and I headed for San Francisco and its charming York Hotel. After learning about the York—and its ghost—from some friends, I had talked by phone to a lady who worked there and arranged a tour.

Located at 940 Sutter Street, this "European-style boutique hotel" was built in 1922 and was completely renovated in 1995. Among its attractions is the Plush Room, a cabaret-style room with a very colorful history. It was here that the hotel opened the Plush Room Cabaret in the Roaring '20s, at the height of Prohibition. A maze of secret passageways led to the popular—and highly illegal—night spot, where many of the top entertainers of the day are said to have performed.

One night in particular stands out in the minds of ghost buffs. When the cabaret lights began to dim, a tall, slender man entered the room. Dressed in top hat and tails, he crossed the stage and sat down at the baby grand piano. Soon the crowded room was swaying to the man's ragtime tunes.

Then, without warning, the music stopped. Suddenly the pianist slumped in his seat, and his head came crashing down on the keyboard! Word is that the man was dead even before his head hit the keys, and that his ghost has haunted the hotel ever since.

Today the Plush Room continues to be a popular (and legal) nighttime attraction—and apparently the pianist is still around, too! His elegantly dressed image has been sighted not only in the cabaret, but also wandering the halls and in the basement. He may even have a companion, as our hostess informed us that the ghostly image of a woman has been observed on the dance floor of the Plush Room, accompanied by a partner who is tall, thin, and well-dressed. As you might guess, he is said to "greatly resemble" the ragtime pianist.

Interestingly, during the last decade a parapsychologist conducted a séance at the establishment in the company of two dozen hand-holding participants (including some skeptics as well as some hotel workers who believed in the ghosts). Reportedly, she was able to summon the ghost of the dead piano player, who described himself as a "song and dance man" by the name of Joseph O'Reilly (not Lester, as he was often referred to by members of the York staff). He also confirmed that he had died at the piano in the 1920s. Although I don't know the reactions of all those who attended the séance, it seems safe to say that some of them left with more than mixed feelings about the experience.

Incidentally, as I learned from the material our hostess provided, the York has yet another claim to fame, that of being chosen as one of the locations for the Alfred Hitchcock film *Vertigo* (as I've already mentioned, that eerie movie also featured the mission of San Juan

Bautista). Thinking back as well to the spooky school-house in Bodega that was used in *The Birds*, I can only surmise that the "master of suspense" had quite a knack for choosing locations with ghostly connections!

As a postscript to this entry, I might mention that before leaving the York I asked our hostess whether she knew about any other ghostly happenings in San Francisco hotels. It turned out that she had worked at several other hostelries in the city, many of which, she indicated, had interesting stories connected with them. The one she chose to share concerned a personal experience at one of the best known of San Francisco's fine hotels, the fabulous Fairmont on Nob Hill.

It seems that over the years several unexplained happenings have taken place at the Fairmont, with the fifth and sixth floors of the hotel's old section being the most active. It was in that area that this incident took place. One day, our hostess related, a co-worker and close friend ran up to her and several other workers in a state of shock. Breathlessly, she blurted out a story about blood (or at least something red) splattered all over the white marble walls and the steps of the staircase that led from the fifth to the sixth floors. Alone when she saw it, she had panicked and exited the area on the run.

Upon hearing this account, everyone raced for the staircase. But when they got to the indicated location, the walls and steps were as pristine as ever. In concluding her story, our hostess shook her head in wonder and said that to this day she doesn't know what her friend could have seen that caused her such a fright.

It was at the grave site that she appeared . . .

June 21, 1999 Recently I learned the details of a strange happening involving the family of a woman I have known for about twenty years, whom I will call Susan. I had first heard about the incident a couple of years ago, by way of a comment Susan made to my wife. When I followed up, Susan agreed to write the story down for me, but it took some time before she was able to gather the information from her aged mother. Today she presented me with a brief written account of a most unusual and memorable affair.

The story concerns one of Susan's paternal uncles, whom I will refer to as Henry. Chinese by birth, Henry departed from China in the 1940s, leaving his first wife behind, and migrated to America. After settling in Sacramento, he married a second woman some twenty years younger than he. (At that time, having more than one wife was not an uncommon practice among Chinese men, many of whom continued to marry until one of their wives produced a son.) Soon Henry had both a boy and a girl. Susan remembers many people assuming that they were Henry's grandchildren.

Meanwhile, Henry's first wife remained in China, where she was very respected and in great demand as a midwife. She was said to be strong-minded, intelligent, and well educated (a rarity for Chinese women at the time). Before coming to the United States, Susan's mother became very close to this formidable lady (her sister-in-law and Susan's aunt by marriage).

By the early 1960s, Henry's first wife had died. Henry himself was in his eighties, and in failing health. One day when Susan's parents were visiting him in the hospital, they witnessed something extraordinary. Also in the room at the time were Henry's second wife and their two children. Suddenly wife number two started hitting the children. Then she began talking what sounded like nonsense in an unfamiliar voice. Almost immediately, however, Susan's mother recognized the voice as that of Henry's first wife, whom she had known so well in China!

Upon making the connection, Susan's parents started talking calmly to the distraught woman, taking pains to address her correctly and with respect—and as if she were wife number one! It was then that the deceased woman, through the lips of wife number two, complained that no one was showing her any respect and that her husband treated her as if she didn't exist.

After hearing her concerns, Susan's father asked what he could do for her. She replied by saying that she wanted her picture to be placed in her husband's house, and both of their names put on his headstone.

With that, things soon returned to normal, and Henry's second wife became herself. True to his word, Susan's father wasted no time in putting a framed picture of wife number one in his brother's house.

The dead woman was not seen or heard from again—that is, not until after Henry died and the family was gathered at the cemetery. It was there, at the grave site, that her image appeared, looking contented and peaceful. She was dressed in white and looked just like Susan's mother remembered her from thirty-five years before.

Oh, yes, Susan's father did keep his second promise, too. Today Henry's remains lie beneath a tombstone inscribed with both his name and that of the wife he had left behind so long ago—and whose own remains sleep peacefully half a world away.

She was attired in a costume of "Edwardian splendor" . . .

June 24, 1999 On a trip to Sacramento for Railfair '99 (a celebration of California's historic railroads), my wife and I decided to work in a visit to the Gold Country. Among other things, I wanted to check out the historic Empire Mine in Grass Valley, about an hour north of the capital city. The Empire Mine is described as the oldest and richest hardrock gold mine in the state, with approximately 5.8 million ounces of gold having been extracted from its 367 miles of underground passages. Today it is open to the public as a State Historic Park.

All this was enough to make the site worth a visit, but—as you've probably guessed—the reason for this note is that the mine is also said to harbor a ghost. To be more precise, the ghost is associated with a "cottage" (actually a stately structure in the style of an English manor) that served as the country home of William Bowers Bourn, Jr., who inherited the mine from his father in 1874. The house and its grounds are to this day a Nevada County showplace. Built in 1897, the building features an exterior fashioned from brick and waste rock from the mine. The interior walls are of heart redwood planed by hand and left in its natural state. The leaded windows were specially designed to withstand the vibrations from the mine's eighty-stamp mill. Not exactly most people's idea of a cottage, the dwelling also includes a wing for the servant's quarters. It was dubbed the "cottage" to set it apart from some of William Jr.'s more elaborate homes, such as his fabulous 43-room Filoli estate, located about twenty-five miles south of San Francisco.

After touring this deluxe country hideaway, I got to talking with one of its docents, a delightful lady who has worked there for more than twenty years. Having received little more than blank stares from other workers in the park when I inquired about ghosts, I was gratified to see her nod knowingly when I asked if she had ever experienced anything "out of the ordinary" in the building. She went on to say that, in addition to hearing a number of strange sounds ("certainly more than creaking floors"), on more than one occasion she had also felt a "presence" that she took to be the spirit of William Bourn, Jr.

The most remarkable ghostly happening that she reported, however, was one that was witnessed by several people. One day, she related, a second docent had her picture taken in the downstairs living room while dressed in a period costume (an old-fashioned maid's outfit, complete with apron and hat). As the picture was snapped, the "maid" stood near a large window that overlooked the front lawn and garden.

When the film was developed and the photo was passed around, all who were present that day, including the lady who shared this tale with me, were shocked by what they saw. Slightly behind and to the right of the "maid" was a second lady. She, too, was dressed in clothes of long ago, but instead of looking like a maid she was attired in an elegant costume of "Edwardian splendor."

No one could remember seeing such a lady in the building, and certainly no one saw her standing behind the "maid" when the picture was taken. To add to the mystery, people knowledgeable about photography checked the film and agreed that it was not a double exposure. Nor did it show any sign of having been tampered with.

So, either my charming informant is very good about making up stories, or something strange is going on at the historic Empire Mine. Incidentally, if you decide to tour the site, you might want to ask one of the docents about the "Tommyknockers" who are said to linger there . . . (and who, some say, are the ghosts of men who have been killed in mining accidents).

Author's Note: A few months after recording this note, I received a letter that mentioned another ghost at the Empire Mine. If you do pay the mine a visit, you might also inquire about the "Screaming Lady" whose lifelike image, legend states, has been seen by several people at the Bourn house. When she appears, her mouth is always open as if in a scream. However, no sounds are ever heard, and as often as not she soon becomes transparent and disappears!

Nevada City's haunted "Castle" . . .

June 25, 1999 After visiting the Empire Mine (see preceding note), my wife and I continued on to the historic Red Castle Inn in nearby Nevada City. Overlooking the "Queen City of the Northern Mines" from its perch high on Prospect Hill, the inn has been known as the "Castle" since the early 1860s. Reaching four stories in height, and built of brick, this Gothic Revival structure—complete with picturesque verandas and Victorian trim—was one of the Mother Lode's most impressive homes in its early days. A century and a half later, it continues to be a "must see" for visitors to Nevada City.

Described as one of the first bed and breakfast lodgings in the state, the Castle has been painstakingly restored both inside and out, and its elegant period furnishings are as much admired as its lovely Gothic architecture. *Country Living* magazine has called it a "uniquely American architectural treasure," while *McCall's* described it as "one of the most charming inns in America." Fittingly, the structure is listed on the National Register of Historic Places.

But what about ghosts you ask? Well, according to *Gold Rush Ghosts,* by N. Bradley and V. Gaddis, "the most amazing ghosts of Nevada City, and the most illustrious, have resided at the Red Castle Inn through a succession of owners, remodelings, and occupants. They are, in a word, content and seem intent on staying through time immortal." The best known of these satisfied spirits seems to be a lady by the name of Laura Jean. As a young woman, Laura Jean was employed as a governess to look after the eleven children in the John Williams family, the original owners of the house. As the children grew to adulthood and left home to forge lives of their own, Laura Jean stayed on to watch over and care for the house. Her stay lasted into old age, until one night she died peacefully in her sleep.

Apparently, though, that was not the end of Laura Jean's association with the house. In fact, according to an account in the *Sacramento Bee*, "Laura Jean seems to think the paying guests who sleep in the beds at the Red Castle are the Williams children. . . . She feels responsible for them, so she tucks them in, smooths their foreheads and sits on the edge of their beds"!

Besides having been known to sit on guests' legs as well as on the edges of their beds, according to a second source Laura Jean also takes pleasure "in playing tricks with the owners and visiting with the guests." Her "tricks" include moving and even hiding objects (usually small things such as the owner's glasses), and opening and closing drawers. As for talking to the guests, certainly one of the best examples took place in a corner room upstairs. This small room has a window that faces west and is warmed by the afternoon sun. It was here that Laura Jean and the children would gather and she would read stories to them. Apparently she misses this as much as she misses the children, and on more than one occasion her presence has been felt in the room. Once she even kept a guest awake during much of her stay by reading to her and playing with the children down the hall. Fortunately, the guest rather enjoyed the experience, even though she had to go home to get some rest!

According to another interesting report, a psychic once visited the Castle and was able to make contact with Laura Jean. In their conversation Laura Jean told her about the reading room and how it was one of her favorites. She also reminisced about how much she enjoyed sitting in a rocking chair in the afternoon sun as she read to the children. Finally, she went on to say how sad she was that the rocking chair had been moved from the room. When the psychic shared this information with the owners, they wasted no time in putting a rocking chair back in the room.

The list of ghostly happenings connected with the Castle includes a great many other incidents as well, such as the sightings of an older man who appeared to be inspecting the workmanship when the building was being restored; the reading-room door that slammed shut when no one was in the room, or even on the same floor; a strange illumination that circled the foot of one of the guest's beds; the figure of a man dressed in black who was seen on the deck after more than a foot of snow had fallen, but who left no footprints in the fresh snow; the sighting of a ghostly soldier in a Civil War uniform (brass buttons and all) in one of the children's rooms; and the apparition of a "sober-faced" fellow attired in a hooded robe who was observed going from one room to another, passing through a locked door on the way.

The account I like best, however, tells about an event that occurred during a New Year's Eve party at the inn. Evidently the party was a costume affair, with guests dressed in Victorian clothing. The party was a great success, and people from town happily mingled with the inn's guests far into the night.

One guest, however, whom I will call Marie, was a nondrinker and was not quite as caught up in the festivities as many of the others. Around midnight, she decided to retire. After climbing the stairs to her room, she prepared for bed and then decided to read a while before going to sleep.

It was while Marie was propped up in bed reading that a stranger wearing a gray dress of Victorian styling entered her room. As if this wasn't odd on its own, the lady was carrying a small dog (resembling a Bedlington terrier). The lady nonchalantly crossed the room and sat at the foot of her bed, chatting pleasantly all the while about the party and other matters. Despite her bewilderment, Marie found herself taking an active part in the conversation. Eventually, however, she grew weary, and the lady in gray stood up to leave. Upon shifting the dog from one arm to the other, she faced the bed and said, "Everything is going to be just fine." With that she left the room and closed the door.

Needless to say, Marie was caught off guard by this mysterious comment and wondered what it might mean. By this time, though, she was so drowsy that she soon drifted off to sleep.

When morning came and the inn's guests assembled for breakfast, Marie looked about for her new friend. Not seeing her in the room, she asked the owner who the lady was who had been dressed in gray and carried a dog. The startled owner replied that no one at the party had brought a dog, and anyone who had done so would have been asked to leave, as dogs were not allowed in the building.

Now, this tale would seem to have a natural explanation, assuming that the midnight visitor and her dog somehow escaped everyone's notice before appearing uninvited in Marie's room. But before you jump to conclusions, consider these intriguing facts. First, Laura Jean frequently is referred to as the "Lady in Gray" because she has often been observed wearing a floor-length gray Victorian dress. Second, she is said to have had a Bedlington terrier when she worked for the Williams family!

In case you still might be wondering whether the story wasn't just made up, let me say that I had mixed feelings about it at first myself. Later, however, I learned that about three years after the current owners acquired the inn, they chanced to see an old acquaintance, now a respected resident of the San Francisco Bay Area, at a charity affair in the East Bay. Naturally enough, the conversation soon turned to Nevada City and the Red Castle Inn. It was then that the owners, much to their astonishment, heard firsthand confirmation of the "Lady in Gray" story. Yes, their old friend was none other than Marie, who until that accidental meeting had no idea that her friends had purchased the property!

Author's Note: If you decide to visit the Red Castle Inn, be sure to stop by Nevada City's picturesque 1860s-vintage Firehouse No. 1. Located on Main Street, the firehouse now houses a historical museum—and, according to a number of visitors as well as published accounts, its own collection of ghosts as well! My favorite story involves a red-haired lady of questionable repute who has been seen at the keyboard of an old piano that was rescued from a Gold Country bordello . . .

The boy was awakened by a strange light . . .

October 11, 1999 In the course of preparing for a talk, I started going through my file of items related to Mission San Antonio and south Monterey County. Among the items I pulled out were some interview tapes I had made back in the mid 1970s of some long-time residents and people who were associated with the aged church. One tape in particular had a tale with a ghostly twist, and after listening to it again after so many years I thought it was just too good a story not to include in this book. Although I've chosen not to list the name of the person who shared this account with me, I will say that he was a member of the mission staff and was a witness to the events that are discussed here.

The story begins in far-off England, where a lady whom I will call Betty had a very vivid dream, unlike anything she had ever experienced before. The dream featured a walled-in garden, or perhaps an inner court, with a well and a vine that grew above the well. God, it seems, wanted Betty to seek out this place.

Unfortunately, nothing in the dream told Betty where the garden might be. Evidently, she believed it was somewhere in the United States, as she went to New York with a traveling companion and began her search. However, after visiting countless communities throughout the United States, she was unable to find the court that she had seen in her dream.

Finally Betty arrived in California and somehow found her way to remote Mission San Antonio. When she walked through the corridor that led to the mission's inner court, she knew at once that she had found the spot she was seeking. There was the walled-in garden, there was the well, and above the well was a grapevine. (The vine, incidentally, was planted by the padres back in the 1770s, and it is still alive and continues to bear fruit.)

When Betty realized she had finally found the place God had wanted her to seek, she asked the church authorities if she could stay. Although the mission was equipped to handle short-term guests, the staff was hesitant to let her stay for an extended period, as her traveling companion had told them that Betty was dying of cancer. The companion herself had to continue on to Los Angeles, and the mission staff did not have the help or the facilities to take care of someone who was gravely ill.

When Betty said that she would stay only for a short time, the staff relented and decided to let her stay. Betty, however, grew progressively weaker and soon was forced to spend much of her time in bed. When it became obvious that she did not have much longer to live, the clergy met with her and told her that they thought it would be best for her to return to England, where she could be with her relatives and be properly cared for. Betty understood their predicament and consented to leave, asking only to be allowed to stay a few more days so that she could attend midnight mass on Christmas Eve. Left unsettled for the moment was the question of who would accompany her on the flight home.

So it was that Betty was able to enjoy the beautiful midnight mass. As coincidence would have it, later on Christmas Day a visitor stopped by the church on a holiday outing. During her tour she happened to mention to one of the clergy (the man who told me this tale) that she was going to Europe and was looking for a traveling companion.

Well, this sounded almost too good to be true, so the clergyman promptly told her about Betty. Undiscouraged by Betty's illness, the lady volunteered to accompany her to England. For her part, Betty was thrilled to have company for her trip, and before long the two travelers bid a fond farewell to the mission and its dedicated staff.

But that, as they say, is only the beginning of the story. Soon after the new year, a group of juniors and seniors from a college in the San Francisco Bay Area came to San Antonio for a "community living" experience. While they were there, the men were housed in one wing and the women in another. One of the young men wound up in the room that Betty had used during her stay.

At two o'clock one morning, the collegian who was sleeping in Betty's old room was awakened by a strange light that "came through his room." It was so bright that it lit up the room as if it were day!

Terrified by the light, the young man became paralyzed with fear and began to perspire all over. After a few seconds the paralysis began to lift as the light slowly faded from view, as if it were going out of the window. When the paralysis was gone, the student jumped from his bed and ran down the hall, yelling and pounding on his neighbors' doors. As you might expect, most of the other students thought he was either high or making the story up. But when he was confronted by the clergy, they realized that he was genuinely shaken. Since no amount of coaxing could persuade him to go back to the room, he was given another place to sleep.

About two weeks later, long after the collegians had left, a postcard arrived from England with the news that

Betty had died. When the clergy checked the date, they were shocked to see that she had died on the same night that the light had appeared in her old room.

And that wasn't all. For the message also indicated that Betty had passed away at *two o'clock in the morning!*

Tales of Alcatraz . . .

October 16, 1999 The island of Alcatraz has a unique history and mystique. Over the years, when I looked out at "the Rock" from the deck of a passing ferry or cruise boat, or simply gazed at it from the shores of San Francisco Bay, I often mused about what life was like for the inmates of one of America's most famous federal prisons. What must have gone through their minds, I wondered, when they looked out at the beautiful San Francisco skyline, knowing that only a short distance away people were free and enjoying life in one of the world's most magical cities? And how many of the tales told about them and their infamous prison were true?

In time my curiosity led to some research about Alcatraz, which in turn led to a few surprises. Among them was the fact that the island's prison was a federal penitentiary for less than thirty years, from 1934 to 1963. Its history as a place of confinement goes back much farther, however—all the way to 1859, when the island was a U.S. Army post and a group of court-martialed military convicts were quartered there. During the Civil War, approximately 100 members of the Confederate navy were imprisoned on the Rock. The next two to three decades saw Indian leaders from various tribes and territories—including proud warriors who refused to give in to the white man—held at the landmark location, along with an assortment of thieves, deserters, rapists, murderers, and the like. In 1898, thanks to the Spanish-American War, prisoners from the Philippines became the latest to experience the Rock's "hospitality."

In the early 1900s Alcatraz again became home to Army incorrigibles. Soon after that the San Francisco earthquake of 1906 opened a fissure on the island. The prison buildings remained intact, however, and were soon used to house the inmates who had been confined at the San Francisco jail, which had suffered severe damage.

Later that decade the Army started construction of new prison buildings, and in 1911 the facility became known as the United States Disciplinary Barracks (in other words, an Army prison). After the United States entered World War I, Alcatraz was used for the containment of Army prisoners as well as seamen who had been impounded from German ships. The period following the war is described by prison historians as a time of disuse and deterioration, as only the most incorrigible Army disciplinary cases were incarcerated at the site.

This brings us to the 1930s and Alcatraz's transformation to a high-security federal penitentiary that would gain international fame as "America's first escape-proof prison" and the home of some of the nation's best-known badmen. Among the most notorious of these was gangster Al Capone. Interestingly, after "Scarface" was incarcerated, he teamed up with three other convicts to form a prison band. With Big Al on banjo and Machine-Gun Kelly on drums, it must have been a "mean" group! However, things weren't all ragtime tunes and good times for the ex-gangland chief, and after several attempts on his life by fellow inmates he was excused from yard privileges for the remainder of his stay.

It goes without saying that a place like Alcatraz is bound to collect some ghost stories, including some that have the feel of legends. Take Capone, for example, whose spirit has been said to haunt the former prison. Big Al spent his last year there in the hospital ward, where he whiled away the hours playing the banjo. By the time he was transferred to another institution, he was near insanity. Ultimately he met his end at a mansion in Florida (which itself is said by some to be haunted). Yet, even though Al Capone didn't die at Alcatraz, in the years since his departure more than one guard has stated that he has heard banjo music coming from the gangster's old cell. Well, who knows? Maybe Scarface was tuning up for an encore performance of the prison band.

Over the years a number of people have been victims of murder or suicide on Alcatraz, not to mention several other inmates besides Capone who went insane while being confined there, particularly in the "hole" (the solitary-confinement cells). So it's perhaps natural that park employees and tourists *have* experienced peculiar goings-on at various locations in the facility. Among the most common of the occurrences are a variety of strange sounds. These range from clanging noises (also described as "clanking metal") that originate in a locked corridor where visitors aren't allowed, the sound of running (or marching) footsteps that sometimes seem to come from the uppermost tier of cells, male voices that can be traced to the old hospital ward, and an eerie scream coming from the "dungeons" where the solitary cells were located.

Other than noises, an assortment of odd feelings have been experienced by workers on Alcatraz. The majority of these "bad vibes" seem to be experienced in or around the "hole." Number 14 seems to be the most ominous of these cells, although cell 12 has its share of tales as well. Among the reports about cell 14 are the feelings of "sudden intensity" that have been experienced there. Some, of course, have blamed such feelings in part on the workers' knowledge of the torture and agony that took place at the site. Perhaps less easily explained is the intense cold that is said to radiate from the cell even on warm days, especially in a two-foot area in one corner where the naked prisoners are reported to have huddled.

Perhaps the best-known ghostly account associated with Alcatraz takes us back to 1946, when an elaborate escape attempt went awry. A number of convicts and guards lost their lives as a result of this incident, including a defiant trio of prisoners who met their end—guns in hand—in a narrow corridor between cell blocks. It is from this utility hall (which housed wires, ventilation ducts, and pipes) that the clanging noises have been heard, and it is here that a psychic picked up on some rather bizarre vibes and graphic mental images suggestive of a long-ago tragedy.

Other than such reports (which include gruesome descriptions of dismembered bodies and such), I could go on with grisly tales that tell of such things as the extreme brutality and psychological torture that are rumored to have taken place on Alcatraz (usually, as one might expect, in the hole). Also of interest to ghost buffs are numerous accounts that tell of such things as feelings of being watched; the choking sensation of smoke in an abandoned laundry room that mysteriously disappears as quickly as it appears; the distinct, if somewhat distant, sounds of voices of tormented souls; bad vibrations suggestive of abuse, mistreatment, fear, and pain; a creature with glowing eyes that haunts certain solitary cells; the appearance of a dead inmate who was counted among the living in a convict line-up, only to disappear before everyone's eyes; the sobbing sounds of a woman coming from the long-abandoned dungeon area; and the appearance of groups of phantom prisoners and soldiers who have been seen by guards, guests, and families who lived and worked on the island. Then there was the sighting at a Christmas party at the warden's house (since destroyed by fire) of the ghostly image of a man with mutton-chop sideburns who wore a gray suit and cap. Several of the party goers, including key prison personnel, saw the apparition before it faded from view. Of special interest to this story is the added information that when the ghost appeared the room turned icy cold, and the fire in the stove went out!

Certainly I could go on with other accounts about Alcatraz, but I think you'll agree that the sampling presented here is enough to establish that the Rock has a most colorful history. And, if we can believe even a few of the ghost-related stories, we will have to admit that the prison seems to have an abundance of supernatural activity.

I should add that the current crop of Alcatraz employees I've been able to contact almost all discount the ghost stories and emphasize that they deal with fact, not fiction. But wherever you stand when it comes to ghosts, if you've ever caught sight of the Rock on a night when fog enshrouds it, or just felt its imposing presence looming in the bay, I think you'll agree that Alcatraz is perfectly capable of creating a spooky atmosphere second to none!

Author's Note: Although I consulted more than a dozen sources and talked with numerous people about Alcatraz and its ghosts, I wish to tip my hat once again to Richard Winer and Nancy Osborn (authors of the book *Haunted Houses*) and thank them for the information I was able to glean from that work.

The show must go on . . .

November 24, 1999 Today brought an end—of sorts—to a "ghost hunt" that began a few weeks ago, while I was in Long Beach for the California Reading Association's annual conference. In chatting with people at the conference who came to hear my talk, I invited anyone who had ghost stories to share about the areas in which they lived to look me up before the conference was over. Although I heard a number of stories over the next couple of days, most were short on detail or substance. One, however, was certainly colorful, and, better still, permitted some follow-up investigation.

The tale came from a graduate of the University of Redlands (located in Redlands, California) and concerned a co-ed who had attended the institution about twenty-five years ago. This young lady was very much involved with the drama department and the various productions they put on. One night, she was rushing back to the campus for the opening-night performance of a play when a dense fog engulfed the road she was on. The result was a terrible accident that took her life. However, true to the tradition that the show must go on, the girl's ghost continued on and arrived at the school's Wallichs Theater before the curtain went up. And, unbeknownst to her fellow performers, or any of the stage crew, her spirit carried on and helped make the opening-night performance a success. Certainly, we can only wonder what went through the minds of the cast and crew when they realized—after the fact—that the actress who performed so well that night was already dead at the time of the performance!

This, at least, is one version of the tale (another suggests that the young woman's ghost worked backstage on that first night). As it happened, at the time I heard this story I was planning to be at another conference in Palm Springs less than two weeks later, and since Redlands was on the way, I knew I would have the opportunity to check it out. After a few phone calls, I was able to set up a meeting with a well-known Redlands historian who is familiar with campus lore.

With high hopes that new details might be in the offing, I contacted the historian soon after arriving in Redlands. He was, indeed, familiar with the tale, and had even known the young woman in question. Unfortunately, instead of adding to the account, he found a number of reasons to debunk it. He seemed most concerned about the distance from the accident site to the theater, suggesting that—assuming there was such a thing as a ghost—the young woman's spirit would have been far more likely to haunt the scene of the tragedy than to find its way to the theater.

That conversation took place a week ago, and it seemed to be the end of the trail as far as the Wallichs Theater ghost is concerned. Today, however, I did learn an additional detail from the person who had first told me the story. As we were talking over the phone (she had returned a call I'd made to check out a few facts), she mentioned that the young woman's ghost was seen on other occasions besides the night when she was killed. At these times her image was most often observed in the wardrobe room.

Despite the doubts of skeptics like the distinguished gentleman I spoke with, in one version or another the story of the ghostly thespian continues to be a popular part of university lore and is often recounted around Halloween in the campus newspaper. If you happen to find yourself on the grounds of the University of Redlands, you might want to look into the Wallichs Theater ghost for yourself. And while you're there, you might also want to check out the reports of ghostly sightings at Grossmont Hall, where another co-ed reportedly died, perhaps by suicide, in one of the dormitory rooms. On several occasions, it is said, her ghost has been seen either in her room or on the balcony outside.

Before ending this note, I'd like to briefly mention a second tale the University of Redlands graduate shared with me, one that also has a connection to the university. Many years ago, it seems, a young boy who attended an elementary school in the hills near Redlands was struck by a car in front of (or near) the school. His body was carried to the nurse's office, where he died. At some point after the accident, students from the university began making trips to the elementary school in the middle of the night. Upon parking their cars they would quietly gather in front of the nurse's office. Then one of the students would knock on the office door and call the boy's name, asking if he could come out and play. The students would then press close to the door and listen. Sure enough, within seconds they would hear a sound described as "a thump and a slide, a thump and a slide" coming from inside the office!

By then the students were usually so scared they would take off on the run. And, as the story ends, even though the nights were still, when they ran across the playground heading for their cars, they often saw the tetherballs swinging wildly as their tethers wrapped around the poles!

No, I don't know whether tetherball was the dead boy's favorite sport, or even whether the sounds were those of someone headed in the direction of the tetherball courts. Nor, for that matter, can I be sure that the first students to cross the playground hadn't struck the tetherballs on their way, further spooking the students who followed behind!

State Street shenanigans . . .

December 5, 1999 While I was exhibiting books at a meeting held on the Asilomar Conference Grounds, one of the attendees told me about a building in Santa Barbara that boasts a great deal of spooky activity. Inasmuch as Santa Barbara is one of my favorite places to visit, and I'm somewhat familiar with the State Street location where the ghosts are said to be, I thought I'd attempt to track a few of the stories down. Here is what I learned.

The building in which the happenings are said to take place has been a State Street landmark for more than a century. Over the years it has been used as a church, a hotel, a theater, a brothel, and a youth hostel. Today it is a popular nightclub known to most locals as Q's.

No one seems to know when the hauntings began, but rumors of ghosts were common before the building became a nightclub. One evidence of that is the reaction of a visitor to Q's who had been familiar with the facility when it was the Savoy Hotel. Commenting on the many alterations that had been made, this individual pointed especially to the changes above the mezzanine, as he remembered that area as being a "hot spot" where much of the out-of-the-ordinary activity had taken place.

As to activity that *still* takes place, several workers have experienced a variety of happenings in various parts of the building. Examples of these are assorted unexplained noises, including mysterious footsteps, doors opening and closing, and the sound of somebody snoring. One employee even claims to have heard her name repeatedly being called!

More dramatic still are accounts of a particular chair that falls from its perch on the bar after it has been placed there for cleaning purposes. Instead of falling straight down, the chair "flies across the room," often coming to rest on the dance floor! This activity, which has been witnessed by more than one person, continues to baffle all who are aware of it.

The ghost or ghosts at Q's are also blamed for various other pranks, including the rearranging of table settings (which are always placed a particular way, as is the custom at the establishment). The most frustrating pranks, however, take place in the keg room, usually on very busy nights. Among the things that happen there is the mysterious shutting off of the pressure valves to the kegs. On one particular night when the valve to the Sierra Nevada keg was shut off three separate times, the bartender had to tape the valve open in order to keep the beer flowing. What makes this more annoying, not to mention mysterious, is that the only entrance to the keg room is through a door in the floor of the bar. Unfortunately, on busy nights the door is usually covered with people, making it difficult to get to, and impossible to open, without anyone noticing. Nevertheless, someone (or something) continues to interrupt the flow of beer, creating a good deal of consternation.

As to sightings, the most frequently observed apparition is that of a man who is said to hang out near one of the pool tables, wearing a red shirt and jeans (so he has been described by all who have seen him). A second type of sighting was made by one of the employees, who reported seeing a ghostly dog in the upstairs portion of the building.

Even though attempts have been made to learn the identity of Q's ghosts, no one has come up with a definite answer. However, I would be remiss not to mention rumors indicating that sometime in the building's dim and distant past a man was killed during a drug deal that went awry. Supposedly his body was pushed out of an upstairs window, and for all anyone knows it may have been the fall that did him in. It has also been reported that two prostitutes were murdered on the third floor when the structure housed a brothel. Perhaps these tragic events help to explain why many of the mysterious happenings take place on the building's upper floors.

So there you have it, a brief report on the shenanigans in one of Santa Barbara's popular State Street attractions. From all reports, it's worth a visit, whether or not you spot any ghosts!

Incidentally, while I was putting the finishing touches on this note, I gave Q's a last call and spoke with one of the managers. In response to my question about recent goings-on, she said that things had been pretty quiet. Then, after a pause, she confided, "But there are sure a lot of creepy feelings around here!"

Author's Note: Although I chatted with several people about Q's, I would like to give a special thanks to Elizabeth Werhane of the *Daily Nexus* newspaper at the University of

California at Santa Barbara. Not only did she go out of her way to help me, but much of the information in this note was gleaned from an article she wrote.

Séances and such . . .

December 18, 1999 Last Monday the third printing of *Ghost Notes* arrived at our Carmel storage facility. When the Consolidated Freightways driver saw the title printed on the cartons, his curiosity got the best of him and he started asking about the book. During our conversation, I soon learned the reason for his interest in ghosts (he even kept a book about haunted houses in the cab of his truck to read on breaks). It seems that his parents used to live in a house where some rather bizarre goings-on took place. After listening to his description of some of the events, I asked whether he would jot down the things he had told me. More than happy to oblige, he went even further and offered to call his two brothers and his mother (his father having passed away) and jog their memories about some of the happenings.

True to his word, today the driver (whom I will call Ned) delivered three pages of handwritten notes to me. What follows is a condensed version of this chronicle.

The house in question was located in a quiet neighborhood in San Jose. Upon purchasing the property in 1980, Ned's family began hearing strange tales about the house from the neighbors. Not only did the dwelling itself seem to have a checkered past, but the people who frequented it were said to be quite "weird."

Ned was not living at home when his family moved in. However, even though in the beginning his parents poohed-poohed the stories, all the talk about the house made quite an impression on his brothers, who were in high school at the time. In part, the neighborhood gossip suggested that the former occupants—who didn't associate with anyone in the neighborhood—were suspected devil worshippers. In this capacity, it was said, they held regular meetings and conducted séances. During these times strange noises (and a lot of shouting) came from the house.

With stories of this sort, not to mention their children's concerns, echoing in their minds, Ned's parents found it hard to discount the incidents they began to experience in the house. As an example, the door to one of their son's rooms began opening by itself each weekday morning at 6:45. At this time the boy would hear soft footsteps coming toward his bed. The first time this happened, he thought his mother was coming into his room to wake him for school. But when he turned over and glanced toward the door, no one was there! Upon jumping out of bed and going into the kitchen, he found his mom, who said she had neither opened his door nor gone into his room. This odd event continued to take place during the week, but on weekends (when there was no school) the ghost apparently took the day off.

Still, it took some personal experiences to convince Ned's mother that there was indeed something going on that defied normal explanations. The first of many such incidents occurred shortly after the family moved in. Ned's mother was in the living room, alone in the house, when she suddenly saw someone walk across the hall near the bedrooms. More concerned than alarmed, she hurried down the hall looking for the person she had glimpsed. But, as was to happen on an almost daily basis for an extended period, there was no one there! On the one occasion when she was able to make out an image, the figure appeared to be that of a woman dressed in a nightgown. As frequently as this occurred, Ned's mother never became used to it. Whenever Ned chanced to visit after one of these incidents had taken place, his mom was always quite "undone" by the experience.

Ned's father—ever the skeptic—was the last member of his family to be convinced. The event that cinched it for him took place one night after he had watched the late news. His wife was already in bed and asleep. Just as he crawled into bed, he heard a loud scream come from within the room! The scream jolted his wife awake, and he bolted from the bed and raced for the light switch. When the lights were turned on, nothing out of the ordinary could be seen. In his notes, Ned comments that neither mom nor dad slept much that night.

Ned finally got the chance to experience the happenings for himself when he stayed at his parents' house for a few months while he was between jobs. Across from his bedroom was a spare room that was seldom used. Other than a few odd pieces of furniture, the room had a table set up with a puzzle on it, as his mother enjoyed working on puzzles.

One day when Ned was home alone and in his room reading, he heard a loud crash coming from the spare room. Running across the hall, he yanked the door open and switched on the light. He was surprised to see that no one was in the room and that nothing was out of place. In fact, as he looked around, he realized that there wasn't anything there that could have made such a loud crash even if it had fallen. Later, when he informed his parents about the incident, he was told that that wasn't the first time something weird had happened in that room—and that it was the very room where the séances had supposedly been held!

In closing, Ned said that his family lived in the house for six years before moving on. But whenever he and his family get together, they still talk about their "haunted" house in San Jose.

Bits and pieces . . .

January 1, 2000 Well, here we are at the start of a new millennium, and despite the fact that I've now written a number of "ghost" books, my files continue to bulge with odds and ends of ghost-related information and stories I've collected over the years. Certainly, some of these accounts are fragmentary at best, while many have been stored in a "to do" folder, awaiting the day when I would be able to research them further.

As I was completing this latest ghostly volume, I leafed through these notes and found several that, abbreviated or incomplete as they may be, might still be of interest to readers of this work. Here, then, is an assortment of bits and pieces that in one way or another you may find "noteworthy." Think of them as accounts that are waiting to be finished, and as reminders of how many stories are still out there, waiting for someone to record them.

A Prunedale poltergeist . . .

The first of these mini-tales takes us to Prunedale, a rural community located on Highway 101, about halfway between Salinas and Watsonville. The source of the story is my current mechanic, though I hasten to add that he is a rare example of his breed. Not only does he own his own shop, but he specializes in servicing and restoring exotic cars from around the world. If you walked into his establishment on any given day, you'd see such vehicles as Bugattis, Delahayes, Lamborghinis, and perhaps a Rolls Royce or two alongside classic American cars bearing names like Stutz, Pierce Arrow, Mercer, Cord, and Packard.

In fact, I only realized how serious my mechanic was about his ghost story (bits of which I'd heard over the years) when he kept one of his best customers waiting while he tinkered under the hood of my car and finished filling me in on the tale of the Prunedale poltergeist. The customer, who had just arrived in his beautifully restored 1935 Frazer Nash Ulster, soon joined in the conversation. Interestingly, the house this story involves had been moved to Prunedale from Monterey in the 1960s to make way for freeway construction. Whether it had a history in its original location that might help account for the strange goings-on was one of the questions that landed this tale in my "to do" file of accounts that needed further research. To date, I don't know the answer, but I do know how insistent my mechanic was about the odd incidents that had taken place in the dwelling.

Of the various happenings he discussed, the one that occurred most frequently involved doors (and cabinet doors) closing of their own accord—usually at the most inconvenient times, as when his arms were full of groceries or other items. As you can imagine, this alone was not enough to convince skeptical friends and family members that anything truly out of the ordinary was going on, although the mechanic swore there was no natural explanation.

Things came to a head one day when the extended family was sitting around the living room discussing the strange happenings. Frustrated by their disbelief, and more than a little irked by some of their comments, my mechanic finally said, "Fine, believe what you want, but when something out of the ordinary does happen, don't say I didn't warn you!"

Appropriately, within seconds after he said this, the coffee table in the living room rose above the shag rug it had been sitting on and moved a distance of about one foot! No one was touching it at the time. Needless to say, several confirmed skeptics who were in the room at the time suddenly developed an avid interest in unexplainable happenings!

Bells in the Santa Lucia Mountains . . .

Both this account and the next one are based on interviews conducted by fourth-grade students as part of the

225

Monterey Peninsula's Memories Shared contest. The contest, which was a spinoff of a local-history book I had written for use in Peninsula schools, was held annually for ten years. One of the four events, and my favorite, was "old-timer interviews." During the decade that the contest ran, the kids collected some fascinating facts and lore from the many old-timers they spoke with.

This first tale, which concerns the sounds of bells in the Santa Lucia Mountains along the Big Sur coast, comes from a pioneer coastal resident who was interviewed in 1990. It is very reminiscent of a couple of stories in my book *Ghostly Tales and Mysterious Happenings of Old Monterey.* One of these accounts tells of bell sounds in the Santa Lucias that can be traced to a tragic accident involving a wagon filled with tanbark that went over a cliff along Mal Paso Creek, killing its driver. The lead horse had bells attached to its collar, and for years after the accident people who used the cliffside trail swore that when they passed the spot where the wagon and its team left the road, they could hear the horse's bells. The second *Ghostly Tales* story is about the unmistakable clatter of a team and wagon racing down the narrow and rut-filled Palo Colorado Canyon Road toward the coastal community of Notley's Landing. Several people are said to have dived for cover to get out of the spirited team's way—only to find themselves staring down an empty road with nary a trace of hoof or wheel prints to be found!

With this background, let me turn to the old-timer's interview as the fourth grader recorded it a decade ago. When the gentleman being interviewed was a young lad (in the early 1930s), he was in the habit of taking his .22 rifle into the foothills of the Santa Lucias to hunt for rabbits. On several occasions, at about 10:00 a.m., he heard the sound of bells. At a loss to explain where the sounds came from, he finally asked his dad about them.

In response, the father indicated that he, too, had heard the bells. He then went on to say that, according to legend, many years ago a stagecoach driver on the Big Sur run had attached bells to his rig so that people could hear him coming from a long distance away. One day, when the coach was high-balling down a hill, something spooked the horses, causing the driver to lose control of his team. Upon rounding a bend at breakneck speed, the coach took a tumble, killing the driver. And, as the story ends, the bells "are the sounds of the stagecoach, and the ghost of the man still driving it."

Now, whether this bit of Santa Lucia lore is connected with either of the accounts I recorded in *Ghostly Tales* is impossible for me to say, as the commonalities (the sound of bells, a tragic accident) are balanced by the discrepancies (for example, if it was the stagecoach that had the accident, what about all the tanbark that was found scattered up and down the creek?). Still, it's ill-fitting pieces like these that make investigating ghost stories a fun challenge!

The ghost of a priest was often seen . . .

The second old-timer's interview takes us to the old Catholic rectory next to Monterey's historic Royal Presidio Chapel. I touched on both of these buildings in an earlier note (see "Unholy happenings at Monterey's Royal Presidio Chapel . . . ," page 90), and certainly both are well known to local ghost buffs.

To appreciate this account it is important to know that from the early 1890s to the late 1920s a popular Monterey priest lived in the upstairs portion of the old rectory. And, according to the old-timer—a well-known and respected Monterey clergyman in his own right—it is the ghost of this priest that was often seen on the rectory's second floor. (Here I might add that, according to other accounts, the priest's ghost was also seen in other parts of the old rectory, as well as in the Royal Presidio Chapel and at Carmel Mission, several miles away.)

What makes the old-timer's comments of particular interest are some additional details that the fourth-grade interviewer elicited. According to this clergyman, who was in a position to know what he was talking about, after the popular priest died he was buried in Los Angeles. Unfortunately, he passed away without saying some of the masses he was supposed to say. It was after his death in 1930 that people claimed to "see a ghost dressed in priest's clothing" in the upstairs of the old rectory, hundreds of miles away, where the good father's rooms used to be. These sightings did not cease until after the masses had been said by fellow priests and the deceased man's remains had been disinterred from their original resting place and moved to the Carmel Mission cemetery, as he had requested before his death. This latter event took place in 1984. It was only then, more than fifty years after the beloved priest's death, that the rectory sightings finally ceased!

Ghostly tales from Santa Cruz and vicinity . . .

With all the accounts in this book that relate to the Monterey area, I would be remiss not to mention at least a few of the hauntings that have taken place in and around the communities at the northern end of Monterey Bay.

Take Capitola, for example. One of the best-known restaurants in this picturesque bayside community, which is known as Shadowbrook, is said to have a ghost. In fact, it may have more than one, as the presence of both a man and a woman have been seen.

The original structure (or what remains of it) dates back to the 1910s and was built as a summer home. Most of the people who are familiar with the facility's hauntings are of the opinion that the male ghost is that of the structure's first owner and builder, E. O. Fowler. Happily, the spirits are of the friendly variety and only add to the romance of the establishment. By the way, the ghosts are not recent arrivals, as back in the 1930s and 40s, when the site was little more than a decaying log cabin, it was known as "the haunted house up the river."

Another haunted restaurant on the Santa Cruz side of the bay is located in the tiny Santa Cruz mountain community of Brookdale, which also happens to be the name of both the restaurant and its lodge. There is some debate about whether this structure was built in the 1920s or some time earlier, but most agree that the lodge and its dining room soon became popular with people from throughout central California and beyond. Over the years many celebrities enjoyed both the food and the bubbling mountain stream that ran through the restaurant, among them such Hollywood luminaries as Marilyn Monroe, Tyrone Power, and Joan Crawford.

Among the many odd occurrences that are reported to have taken place at Brookdale are doors slamming shut, televisions and jukeboxes turning on, and the pungent odor of gardenias following workers from room to room. However, the most often discussed activities seem to be related to a young girl who, legend states, disappeared one afternoon more than three quarters of a century ago. She was the niece of the proprietor, and sadly, her body was found several hours later at the bottom of the brook.

The girl's name was Sarah, and she is said to have been about eight years old when the tragedy occurred. Since then, a number of people over the years have claimed to see the image of a young girl, with some saying that she was dressed in early 1900s attire, and others that her clothes had more of a 1940s look. Her image is described as very lifelike, not "hazy," as some people describe ghosts. In addition, her laughter and "cryptic cries" have often been heard.

At one point a well-known psychic was called in to do a "house blessing," and since then things are said to have subsided somewhat. Of course, this all depends on who you talk to, as according to a gentleman I chatted with in 1996 (when I visited the site), out-of-the-ordinary events continue to happen. Among these occurrences is the sighting by one of the current owner's adult daughters of a young girl's ghost walking through one of the walls. A further indication of continued activity is provided by a newspaper article of October 1997, which states that guests sometimes still leave the lodge prematurely, "citing such things as strange visions and auras."

The coastal community of Santa Cruz also boasts its share of ghosts. For openers, a tale with a touch of history takes us to the site of the Mission of the Holy Cross (Santa Cruz). This church was established in 1791 as part of Alta California's original mission chain. One of its early padres, Father Andres Quintana, is often said to have been cruelly murdered in 1812. However, because so many questions have been raised over the years about the cause of his death—and who was to blame—legend states that his spirit still wanders the hill where the mission first stood . . . and will continue to do so until the truth is known. Incidentally, this story comes from a family who have lived on Santa Cruz's "Haunted Hill" (the site of the original church) for more than 150 years, some of whose members claim to have personally encountered Father Quintana's ghost.

Speaking of hills, did you know that our old friend Alfred Hitchcock patterned the "freaky" Bates Motel in his classic thriller *Psycho* after the ominous-looking McCray hotel on Santa Cruz's Beach Hill? And, yes, a ghost has been reported at the McCray (also spelled McCrary).

An even better-known haunt on Beach Hill is the palatial Golden Gate Villa (since renamed Palais Monte Carlo), which was constructed by Major Frank McLaughlin, a one-time partner of Thomas Edison. This Queen Anne-style structure has looked over the town and its pristine beaches for more than one hundred years. Built in the early 1890s, the 23-room mansion has been the scene of numerous gatherings, and has played host to many famous people, notably Theodore Roosevelt. Not only was Roosevelt a good friend of McLaughlin, but the elegant old edifice boasted a special Teddy Roosevelt Room. And, in keeping with the Roosevelt theme, the downstairs dining room is said to have been "wallpapered" with elephant hides (a gift to McLaughlin from Teddy).

Sadly, even though Major McLaughlin experienced many highs in his life (including offers to run for governor of California and to serve in President McKinley's cabinet), he also sank to terrible lows. It was during one of these lows—two years to the day after his wife died—that he went to his stepdaughter's room and shot her in her sleep. He then went downstairs and drank a suicide cocktail of lemon juice and strychnine (or lime juice and cyanide, take your pick). Included in his suicide note was a macabre final request: Would his doctor please chloroform the family cat?

Today a "lavender-dressed spirit" is said to float about the building. As you might guess, she is thought to be the ghost of McLaughlin's lovely stepdaughter, who died at his hand.

Certainly the McLaughlin mansion isn't the only Santa Cruz Victorian that boasts a ghost. Longtime residents can tell you about the "white lady's house" (so named because of the female occupant's pale complexion and filmy gossamer gown) that was located near the old cemetery. Unfortunately, the building burned down approximately thirty years ago, and, some people say, its ghost also went up in smoke. Another structure that is said to be haunted is the beautiful, more than century-old Eastlake-style edifice with a Queen Anne tower and witch's cap that is located on California Street. Then there is the ghost of Sarah Cowell (or is it a heavy equipment operator?) that frequents the Upper Quarry or Haunted Meadow area of the University of California at Santa Cruz.

231

The list could go on and on, but I think I'll bring these musings about Santa Cruz to a close with a brief account of a ghost in an old house at what locals refer to as Red, White and Blue Beach (a few miles north of town). The dwelling in question is a two-story farmhouse that has been around for nearly a century and a half. Among the happenings reported at this aged structure are mysterious footsteps, doors that slam shut, and the sounds of crystal shattering (though no broken glass can be found). There is also a story of a guest who was awakened by a rooster crowing, when no rooster was actually there . . . even though the guest could plainly see its outline on the arm of a couch. A number of objects have been involved in less noisy manifestations, including perfume bottles that dance, beds that shake, covers that are pulled from people who are trying to sleep, drawers that open, pictures that fly off walls, and plants and wine glasses that move on their own, sometimes almost hitting people or spilling their contents on them.

The number of such reports certainly causes one to wonder who, or what, is creating all the confusion. A number of people have investigated the site, including several well-known psychics and the author of a second book on California ghosts, and all have their own theories. For my part, I like to think that the culprit is none other than the ghost of the sea captain who had the house built back in 1857. And, in fact, a likely-looking ghost *has* been seen by many people. More than fifty years ago, an aged rain slicker and cap, like those a sea captain might wear, were found hanging on a hook on the back porch when a couple moved into the house. Since then, sightings of the ghostly image of an old sailor (or sea captain) sporting a slicker and cap have been reported by "at least a dozen people a year."

There is even more to the story, so if you're interested, I suggest you check out Antoinette May's book *Haunted*

Houses and Wandering Ghosts of California and read the chapter on the "Red, White and Blue Beach."

A Pacific Grove haunt . . .

I suppose it's fitting, as I near the end of this book, to return to my own neighborhood, the beautiful Monterey Peninsula. After all, as I've commented before, it seems that stories of the supernatural keep finding me even when I'm not looking for them.

This next tale is a good example, as it comes from a fellow (I will call him Jim) who was working as a waiter in a popular Pacific Grove restaurant when I first met him. Eventually, it was Jim's wife, Jan, who wrote up the account of his experiences.

According to Jan's notes, it all began when the couple moved into a small Victorian house near the Pacific Grove shore. Even though they lived in the house for about a year and a half, Jim never felt comfortable there. Things seemed fine during the day—except for a plant in the living room that appeared to move on its own—but at night he always felt like he was "being watched," as if a "presence" was peering at him from the doorway (or, to be more accurate, from around the doorjamb).

The presence made Jim so nervous that it was extremely difficult for him to sleep. In fact, the feelings became so intense that when he went to bed he would always lay with his head facing the door. On one occasion, after he had finally managed to fall asleep, he awoke with the feeling that the presence had moved into the room and was hovering over him!

Apparently Jim wasn't alone in sensing something peculiar in the house, as at about three o'clock each morning their dog woke up and howled "one long, spine-chilling howl." The dog was always in the dining room when it howled, and was always looking into the corner.

One Christmas season when Jim and Jan were out of the area, one of Jim's male friends stayed in the house and took care of the dog. Jim hadn't said anything to his friend about the ghost. However, after picking up some strange vibes, and having the dog repeatedly wake him up during the night with its chilling howls—not to mention seeing a light mysteriously turn on each time the dog howled—the house sitter contacted Jim and Jan and told them that he wouldn't be able to stay the rest of the time. "Something weird" is going on in the house, he complained, and went on to say that it was "definitely" haunted.

Similar incidents and feelings of presence were also experienced independently by two additional male friends, with most occurring in the second bedroom. One friend (who, like the other two, refused to stay in the house ever again) also said that there was "an old woman sewing in the corner."

You may have noticed that it was only the men who complained of being bothered in the house. This pattern was confirmed by the woman who had lived in the house previously to Jim and Jan. Her husband had also experienced feelings of presence, she said, even though she, like Jan, had never felt anything. Moreover, one Thanksgiving when Jan's parents came to visit, her father had an "unsettling feeling" immediately upon entering the house for the first time and felt the hair on the back of his arms rise. Nothing had been said to either him or his wife about a ghost, and Jan's mom had no such feelings.

Upon checking with the Pacific Grove Heritage Society, Jim and Jan learned that no deaths or other unfortunate events had been reported that might explain any "bad vibrations" in the house, let alone why they should only be felt by men. So, as with so many such stories, the possible causes remain a mystery. Meanwhile, I'm left to wonder when the next ghostly account will show up out of the blue as I'm enjoying a meal or a cup of coffee in one of my local "haunts"!

A Stevenson House encore . . .

I can't think of a better way to end this book of notes than to return to one of the most famous haunted houses in California's first capital city, the Robert Louis Stevenson House. If nothing else, this brief tale will demonstrate that, contrary to what some local history buffs believe, Stevenson House ghost stories have been around for a long time.

I first heard about this episode from a Carmel Valley librarian I met in April of 1999. Through her, I was led to a native Montereyan in his seventies who said that he had seen a female ghost at the aged adobe several times in his youth. Interestingly, the star of his story was not the building's famous Lady in Black, but just the opposite—a woman garbed all in white.

When he was a lad back in the 1930s, he explained, he often took a shortcut to school through the backyard of the Stevenson House, which at the time was quite shabby. On perhaps five or six occasions, when he neared the back steps of the building, he saw a lady standing by the door looking at him. She was always dressed in a long, white, "turn of the century" dress. He remembered her as having dark hair, and guessed that she was in her thirties or forties. At the time he assumed that she lived at the site, and didn't think much more about it.

It wasn't until many years later, when he was talking with some friends about the Stevenson House, that he mentioned his boyhood experiences. Upon hearing his description of the lady in white, one of his friends blurted out, "That was no lady, that was a ghost!" It was then he learned that the aged adobe had been empty at that time, and that no one—let alone a lady dressed in turn-of-the-century clothing—had lived or even worked in the building.

With that, he could only look back and wonder just who or what he had really seen. If it was a ghost, he feels sure it was a friendly one, as he distinctly remembered waving to her one day as he passed, and how she prompt-ly waved back.

And so this book comes to an end with yet another question to add to the ever-growing list. Was it a ghost that this elderly Montereyan saw so many years ago? I don't know, but I do know that the stories about the Stevenson House, and many other sites in California, just keep com-ing. Now, it would be easy for a single individual, or a group of people, to come up with some outlandish tale, though even then I've met too many people who were too clearly sincere for me to dismiss their stories out of hand. But when dozens of people, unbeknownst to each other and often unaware of any "ghostly" associations connect-ed with a certain place, *independently* describe events and experiences that have no obvious natural explanation . . . well, then I can only scratch my head and wonder.

What about you? Are you willing to accept even one of the stories you've read as being beyond "earthly" explana-tion? Remember, all it takes is one . . . and you and I will both be forced to confess that there is more going on in our world—and perhaps in another world beyond our ken—than we might care to think . . .

Postscript

March 20, 2000 If you had asked me last week, or even yesterday, whether I was going to write another book about ghosts—say, something like *More California Ghost Notes*—I probably would have shook my head and said no, seven ghost books are enough. Don't get me wrong— it's not that I'm tired of writing about ghosts, or that I'm afraid I'd run out of stories. It's just that after thirty years of dabbling with the strange and unexplained, I can't help but think that it's time for me to take some of my other writing projects off the back burner and bring them to fruition.

However, in this morning's edition of the *Monterey County Herald* there was an interesting feature about "Things That Go Bump in the Night." Included in the section was an article about me entitled "Local Writer in Search of Ghosts." Well, even before I left the house for my morning coffee and bagel, the phone started ringing and people wanted to talk about ghosts. If anything, it was even crazier at the bagel bakery, as several people stopped by my table to comment on the article, share a ghost story, or attempt to line me up for a speaking engagement.

What has all this got to do with another ghost book? Well, I must confess that some of today's tales were quite interesting, and it would certainly be a shame if no one recorded them. For example, one of the accounts was about the ghost of a nurse who had died at the old Monterey hospital. Another was about a mysterious happening at Monterey's old train station. There was even a story about a ghost that had traveled (or "been transported," according to the teller) all the way from England and was now residing in sunny Carmel Valley. Add these accounts to a handful of other tales I've recently acquired, and I must admit that it's hard not to start thinking about another ghost book.

So, regardless of what I might have said yesterday or last week, I'd like to leave the door slightly ajar and say that maybe—provided, of course, that the stories keep coming—another book of similar size may someday see the light of day. If that's something you'd like to see, and if you have a California ghost story that you'd like to share, drop me a line in care of Ghost Town Publications:

Randall A. Reinstedt
Ghost Town Publications
P.O. Drawer 5998
Carmel, CA 93921

Who knows? Maybe together we can make it happen, and maybe this time we won't have to wait ten years for another Ghost Notes book to be published.

Finally, I'd like to close this postscript by thanking you for your interest, and for reading this book all the way to its end. Most of all, I'd like to once again thank everyone who has shared a story, or in their own special way helped to bring this book to completion.

Happy haunting . . .

Acknowledgments

To many people, it must seem that the acknowledgments are the easiest part of a book to write. But with a book like this—which has been in the works for ten years and which depends on input from people for much of its content—writing the acknowledgments poses something of a challenge. After all, it's the people who have shared their experiences with me or turned me on to a particular tale who are the real authors of this work. Whether they wrote me a letter, contacted me by phone, stopped me on the street, buttonholed me at a conference or lecture, or met me for coffee, it is their stories that make this book what it is. They are the ones who opened the door to scores of little-known incidents and strange happenings, many of them never before captured in writing. It is for this reason that I'm listed on the cover as the "recorder" of these accounts, rather than as their author.

Before thanking by name all those who contributed to the writing of this book, I'd like to mention some other sources to which I am also indebted. In tracking down information about people, places, and events, I consulted a variety of written sources, many of which I located in libraries throughout the state. Among the most important of these were old newspaper and magazine articles. Also of interest were such things as aged advertising and promotional brochures and pamphlets. With the help of friends, I also located valuable information on the Internet.

Among the several books I consulted, I'd like to single out a few that were particularly helpful. Two of them would certainly be of interest to anyone who would like to further pursue the subject of California ghosts. They are *Ghost Stalker's Guide to Haunted California*, by Richard Senate, and *Haunted Houses and Wandering Ghosts of California*, by Antionette May. However, I owe my greatest debt to *Haunted Houses*, by Richard Winer and Nancy Osborn, a book that is about more than just the Golden State. I'd also like to thank Richard for sharing some of his knowledge and experiences with me in person when we met back in 1981.

This brings me to the many other people without whom this book would not have come to be. Although I can't thank them enough, here's a heartfelt salute to Manuel Alonzo, Nacharl Anderson, Polly Archer, Theresa Arnott, Brother Timothy Arthur, Barbara Baker, Fernando Batista, Lowell H. Beachler, Debbie Bechler, Marcie and Joe Biagi, Jay Campbell, Barbara Carter, Robin Cauntay, David Charles, Jennifer Cirelli, Miguel Dominguez, Brittany Downing, Bev Ferrito, Sonia Fetherston, Karin Fielding, Margaret Frank, Amber Fry, George Groves, Sally Hamilton, LaVerne Hancharick, Alicia Harby, Ellie Hattori, John Hayashida, Julie Johnson, Michelle Kazeminejod, Ed Larsh, Myrtle Leaman, Cynthia J. Levy, Larry Little, Maniko Lofink, Frank Lucido, Jeanine Manfro, Ray and Barbara March, Scott McKenna, Greg Miller, Charles Moller, Barbara Moon, Kristy and Matthew Murray, Lillie Negron-Tokumoto, Tom Nelson, Margot Petit Nichols, Patty Northlich, John Oliveria, Kent Oren, Mary Beth Orser, Joseph C. Panetta, Ellen Pastore, Jo Ann Perkins, Jan Pisciotta, Ollie Plante, Randy Reed, Carolyn Rice, Teressa Russell, John Sanders, Beverly Kehoe Shea, Steve Staiger, Deyanne Sylliaasen, Maria Tarabbia, Wendy Troutman, Nadine Tugel, Jane Way, Mary Louise Weaver, Elizabeth Werhane, Richard Winer, and Teri Wiseman.

In some cases, I obtained only a first name, or have been requested to withhold a last name. The following people, however, deserve a full measure of thanks as well: Albert, Alice, David, Diane, Herb, Ian, Katherine, Linda, Lorna, Maria, Richard, Sally, Simon, Susan, Theresa, Tom, Tonya, and Wayne.

The next name on my list is certainly one of the most important. With a sharp mind, and an even sharper pencil, my editor, John Bergez, was able to whittle away at a manuscript that was half again as big as the final book. Thank you, John, for your patience and input, and most of all for helping to whip this book into shape.

Let me say to anyone whose name I have inadvertently left out that any such omissions are unintentional. Please accept my apology for the oversight, and my sincere thanks for your contribution.

Finally, I would like to thank my son, Erick, and his wife, Mary Ann, for encouraging me to complete this book even when I wasn't sure quite where it was going. And to my wife, Debbie, what can I say? Thanks for being there through it all, thanks for listening to my tales of woe, thanks for the afternoon cups of coffee, and thanks for helping with the research and snooping through all those clippings files. Not only are these people my family, but they are also my best friends.

Photo Credits

These pages constitute an extension of the copyright page. All photos are the property of their respective owners and are reproduced here by permission.

Page 109: Whaley House photo by Jack E. Boucher, 1960, courtesy Historical Shrine Foundation. The Winchester Mystery House photo is from an old postcard.

Page 110: Hotel del Coronado photo courtesy California History Room, California State Library, Sacramento. Claremont Hotel photo by R. A. Reinstedt.

Page 111: Hotel Del Monte photo by C. W. J. Johnson, courtesy U.S. Naval Postgraduate School Museum. Inset photo by R. A. Reinstedt.

Page 112: Union Hotel photo courtesy Plumas County Museum, Quincy. National Hotel photo by Rich Miller, courtesy National Hotel.

Page 113: Red Castle photo courtesy Mary Louise Weaver. Empire Cottage photo by R. A. Reinstedt.

Page 114: Photo by Greg Kinder, courtesy Governor's Mansion State Historic Park.

Page 115: Photos of The Victorian restaurant building courtesy JoAnn Perkins. Falkirk Mansion photo by R. A. Reinstedt.

Page 116: Main photo by R. A. Reinstedt. Inset showing a scene from *The Birds* is taken from a postcard.

Page 117: Photos by R. A. Reinstedt.

Page 118: Photos by R. A. Reinstedt.

Page 119: Photo by R. A. Reinstedt.

Page 120: Photo by L. Blaisdell.

Page 121: Photo by L. Blaisdell.

Page 122: Photos by R. A. Reinstedt.

Page 123: Photos by R. A. Reinstedt.

Page 124: Photos by R. A. Reinstedt.

Page 125: Photos by R. A. Reinstedt.

Page 126: Inset top right photo by W. Morgan. Other photos by R. A. Reinstedt.

Page 127: Point Pinos photo by R. A. Reinstedt. Battery Point Lighthouse photo courtesy Del Norte County Historical Society Photograph Collection. Inset photo by Mary Lou Saunier.

Page 128: Photo courtesy Queen Mary Seaport Marketing Communications.

Page 129: Photo courtesy Pat Hathaway Collection of California Views, Monterey, CA.

Page 130: "Frank's" photo courtesy Moss Beach Distillery. Other photos by R. A. Reinstedt.

Index of Names and Places

*Page numbers for photographs are in **boldface**.*

Books by Randall A. Reinstedt

Regional History and Lore Series . . .
bringing the colorful history of California's Central Coast to life for adults and older children:

California Ghost Notes
From Fisherman's Wharf to Steinbeck's Cannery Row
Ghost Notes
Ghostly Tales and Mysterious Happenings of Old Monterey
Ghosts, Bandits and Legends of Old Monterey
Ghosts and Mystery Along Old Monterey's Path of History
Ghosts of the Big Sur Coast
Incredible Ghosts of Old Monterey's Hotel Del Monte
Monterey's Mother Lode
Mysterious Sea Monsters of California's Central Coast
Shipwrecks and Sea Monsters of California's Central Coast
Tales, Treasures and Pirates of Old Monterey

History & Happenings of California Series . . .
putting the story back in history for young readers:

Lean John, California's Horseback Hero
One-Eyed Charley, the California Whip
Otters, Octopuses, and Odd Creatures of the Deep
Stagecoach Santa
The Strange Case of the Ghosts of the
    Robert Louis Stevenson House
Tales and Treasures of California's Missions
Tales and Treasures of California's Ranchos
Tales and Treasures of the California Gold Rush

For information on purchasing books contact:

Ghost Town Publications
P.O. Drawer 5998 ♦ Carmel, CA 93921 ♦ (831) 373-2885
www.ghosttownpub.com